The Heart's Townland

marking boundaries in Ulster

Edited by

Brian S Turner

Published by The Ulster Local History Trust
in association with The Cavan-Monaghan
Rural Development Co-operative Society
2004

**EU Programme
for Peace and Reconciliation**

*Funded By ADM/CPA under the EU
Peace II programme and part financed by
the Irish government under the National
Development Plan 2000-2006.*

Designed by April Sky Design
Printed by W&G Baird

ISBN 0 9542832 1 X

Ulster Local History Trust
Box 900
Downpatrick
County Down BT30 6EF

Photographs:
Christopher Hill, cover and pp 8, 10, 11, 14,
15, 16, 17
Crown Copyright, reproduced by courtesy
of the Ordnance Survey of Northern
Ireland, pp 49, 50, 51, 52
Patrick Duffy, p 19a
Alfai Ó Dincin, back cover and pp 47, 58, 68,
77, 82, 124, 125, 126
Brian Turner, pp 19b, 100, 109

Contents

Foreword

Cavan-Monaghan Rural Development Co-operative Society is delighted to have had the opportunity to work in partnership with the Ulster Local History Trust in the organisation of the conference which is given a permanent record in this book. It touched on many aspects of our concern for the development of rural Ireland in the twenty-first century.

The diverse range of speakers explored the tangible and intangible nature of our most basic land division, the townland. Through art, literature, history, folklore, and cartography, people from both sides of our political border addressed thought-provoking themes and issues that led us to a deeper understanding and appreciation of locality and place. We often do not appreciate the richness that we have inherited, and the contributors to this conference emphasised the townland as a uniquely Irish, and useful, feature of our past and present society. In doing so, they reflected both their passion for their own work and a recognition of the importance of place and cultural diversity that is common to all.

The Ulster Local History Trust is to be commended for its proactive approach to local studies, which have wide significance beyond the conference hall. In associating itself with this work the Cavan-Monaghan Rural Development Co-op Society would also like to remember Anthony Leddy, our former chairman who passed away in January of this year. Anthony will be remembered for his passion, enthusiasm and commitment to a better future for rural areas. His ideals and beliefs, which have been recognised by many decision-makers of our time, will live as a legacy and testament to the enormous contribution he has made and the positive effect he has had on so many. We also thank ADM/CPA and the European Union Peace II Programme for ongoing funding of our Heritage Awareness programme in Cavan and Monaghan.

With speech, music and drama from people of all ages, the Heart's Townland conference kept up a sustained momentum. May this book carry its ideas into the future.

Allen McAdam

Manager, Cavan-Monaghan Rural Development Co-op Society Ltd
The Agricultural College, Ballyhaise
County Cavan
2004

Introduction

In the evening my uncle, Dawson Cairns of Ardmeen, used to lean on the gate in the corner of the yard. He smoked his pipe and looked down over the farm. Mostly he said nothing. Sometimes there would be a small boy beside him, who had to climb up the gate to lean on its top.

After a while I realised that my uncle was looking at everything. The corn growing; the moiley cow that hadn't been well; the state of the stone-faced bank with the thorn hedge opposite; the sheep grazing on Aunt Betty's wee farm in Ballynaloan, just where it marched his land in Drumclamph; Sandy Walsh getting home to his house at the Crew bridge. Hardly moving, we could see the detail of the Derg valley existing round our feet and spreading seamlessly out and on to the blue hills of Donegal.

One day my uncle suddenly explained to me why the fields of the farm were shaped the way they were. He talked about the clearing of the land and how the ground underfoot and the ploughing points in the landscape had produced the network of fields and lanes and sheughs and ditches and boundaries which I had explored without understanding. He knew where he was. And back in the house were the postcards from relatives in Arizona and Adelaide, and the yellowing photographs of Sioux encampments where great uncle Willie had lived in his youth.

This book is not about one place, or one memory. It is about appreciating the delicate complexity of the environment we have inherited, country and town, and encouraging development without heedless destruction. Our land is losing its meaning, and with that comes yet another shove in the direction of disharmony with ourselves, as evidenced in the increasing gracelessness with which we treat our surroundings. By concentrating on the meanings of our unique Irish townlands, historical, administrative, and psychological, we intend to assert a view of our landscapes as spaces which give us life, rather than blanknesses to be crossed in getting to somewhere else. It's an increasingly challenging ambition, and it requires hard heads as well as soft hearts.

The second Ulster Local History Trust conference for local historians and community groups took place in Monaghan on 14 and 15 November 2003. It was called 'The Heart's Townland: marking boundaries in Ulster'. In recording its proceedings we must first acknowledge our Ulster poet, Roy McFadden (1921-1999). When we began to formulate ideas for the conference the title of his poem 'The Heart's Townland' caught both our attention and our intention. It gave its name to a volume of his early poems published in 1947, the dust jacket of which made the modest claim that 'he writes well of his own country.' In trying to catch the indefinable with the practical net of townland boundaries we are trying to do the same.

Pat Loughrey's keynote paper addresses the theme with both subtlety and humour. His personal account of a Donegal upbringing combines the greatest intimacy of knowledge with the slight feeling of otherness which often stirs up the best local historical observation. From his current position at the head of the BBC's regional broadcasting in the United Kingdom, he encourages people to be confident about what they know of their own localities, and neither to be intimidated by 'professionals' nor afraid to learn from everywhere. Paddy Duffy's generous work on the evolution of the landscape of south Ulster has contributed much to the foundation of modern townland studies. Here he explains the origin and evolution of townlands from the position of an academic who also knows the contours of his own place. Eugene McCabe, whose distinction as a writer has carried his work far beyond the boundaries of his own townland, is still planted there, surveying the Irish political border, but also transcending all borders with a sweep of observation about locality which takes in, among others, Homer, Virgil, the Book of Kings, Chaucer, Shakespeare, Joyce, Kavanagh, the price of strong bullocks in Cavan, and a return to Corranny. Our former chairman, Jack Johnston, draws on deep practical experience to demonstrate the essential value of townlands for anyone who seeks to study, to understand, and to find their way around, Irish history. His consistent ploughing of this furrow along and across the Ulster border has done incalculable good.

As with our previous conference on 'The Debateable Land' in 2001, it was important that a wide variety of people gave news or information on different aspects of the subject, and these 'short stories' were a characteristic part of the proceedings. No less so were the singers and other musicians, the children who provided drama, and the booksellers and exhibitors. They all contributed to a gathering which contained a diversity and a unity which is familiar to the local history movement but still surprises those whose view of Ulster is formed by the broadcast news bulletins.

There is much more that could have been said about both the music and the clabber of our townlands. That is as it should be. The last chapter of the book, by Bryonie Reid, does not come directly from the conference, but from her academic research into the years of identity crisis in Ulster. In discussing the concerns and activities of those dismayed by the threat to the use and continued meaning of townland names she provides valuable context for much of the rest of the book and demonstrates other directions for analytical thought about these issues.

The contributions recorded here are as varied as their subject, and the personalities of the authors and performers. Our serious purpose involved entertainment, information, humour, instruction and inspiration. Consequently, in trying to put the whole book together in a coherent form I have also left the contributors to speak in their various voices. While a sense of foreboding cannot be excluded from any observation of Ireland at the present time, we choose to offer their positive and civilising concoction.

Of course there is an agenda behind all this. It is gentle and polite. The Ulster Local History Trust believes in the value of exploring our history in a humane and accessible manner, and we relate our purpose directly to the social and political troubles and challenges of our time. Attitudes to our unique inheritance of townlands, those small areas which identify both land and people, and which provide such historical continuity, are just one indicator of our cultural self-confidence, or lack of it. How we treat them in an age of computerisation can provide us with an opportunity to demonstrate that technology can be used to enhance rather than destroy our cultural heritage, and to protest that management without knowledge and empathy does not inspire respect. Our historic names and their meanings are as valuable as our historic monuments and buildings, and all the other environmental inheritances that we need to conserve for their practical use in the present and future.

The Ulster Local History Trust is pleased to have co-operated with the Cavan-Monaghan Rural Development Co-operative Society in producing the Heart's Townland conference and publication. Such collaboration suits the spirit of both bodies. We are grateful to the CMRD's manager and board of directors, and their funders, for their support, and we particularly thank CMRD's Heritage Officer, Niamh McGrath, and her team for all the work which resulted in a job well done.

Brian S Turner
Lisban, Saul
County Down
April 2004

In the secret heart: children's graveyard at Ray. (Photo: Christopher Hill)

The Heart's Townland

Patrick Loughrey

> I greet you now,
> Townland stooked beneath the hill, stored, starred
> With pieces of me.
>> Roy McFadden, *'The Heart's Townland'*

Come now in fancy to north-east Donegal, on the shores of the Swilly, to my heart's townland. It is only one of many thousands in Ireland but it was all the world to me.

Only the parochial is truly universal. As Tipp O'Neill said, 'All politics is local.' Even big businesses think global but act local. It's an irony of the global village that local is becoming ever more important. My new world of BBC broadcasting is becoming ever more local too, and I'm going to talk local now.

First a quotation from John Hewitt's poem 'Ulster Names':

> The names of a land show the heart of the race;
>
> They move on the tongue like the lilt of a song.
>
> You say the name and I see the place –
>
> Drumbo, Dungannon, or Annalong
>
> Barony, townland, we cannot go wrong.

For me it is Drumherrive, Glenalla, Garrygort - Ballyboe, Daraheel, Drumacloghan, Ballyconnolly, and my own beloved Ray, which is half-way between the towns of Rathmullan and Ramelton.

These are my heart's townlands. They surrounded me like pillars of my childhood. They supported my sense of self and underpinned my view of the world. People and their places are inextricably linked. When asked who you were, the answer was simple - Sheridan of Craig, McFadden of the Loops, or McConnell of the Ballyboe. That said it all. If you'll indulge me, those townlands will be my subject as I try to make a few wider points.

Growing up in north-east Donegal the townland of Ray was my home ground, my starting point, a wonderland of mystery. Looking back, maybe it meant more because I was an adopted child, an only child, an outsider, with elderly parents steeped in the way life was. In their stories the Tuatha Dé Danann, the Danes, redcoats, rebels and landlords all merged into a mysterious space, called 'the past'. The epic tale of Irish history seemed to be compressed into the four or five square miles around home.

I know now that there was nothing unique about our townlands and that every parish has its own deep well of tradition. But that's not how it felt then. In a two room thatched house I felt rich, part of something proud and venerable, and that mine was a special place.

Ray (pronounced a bit like 'rye') takes its name from Gaelic *'rath'* – a fort. This refers to the ruins of a circular fort just behind our house. The surrounding wood was called the forth, the field was the cashel, and the townland name meant 'rath', so there were lots of clues. It was a so-called Danish fort from which a tunnel was believed to lead to Lough Swilly and far away. I searched for the entrance to that tunnel and sought its echo for countless happy days, knowing that golden treasure awaited me.

My grandfather claimed to have found, while digging turf on Ray Hill, the intact remains of an ancient warrior, still proudly holding his sword. All had blown away as dust when exposed to the air – gone, lost forever.

More than a century before, the forth had become a cemetery for un-baptised children – part of the Catholic belief in limbo. It was no burial ground, because re-enacting ancient rites, there was no burial. The little body was left on the surface and surrounded by a cairn of stones. I knew the parents, brothers and sisters of children who'd been left there; always before sunrise and always without religious ceremony. Like me, they didn't quite belong.

When she was still at school my grandmother woke one morning to find the garden next to our house had been mistaken for the forth. A tiny body wrapped in silk lay beneath stones. She always said whoever owned it had nothing to be ashamed of, because the body was wrapped in silk. The next morning her father moved that body to join countless others in the forth.

Around that site I found the foundations of the cashel, and a crudely cut cross enclosed in a circle, marking a father's last tribute. It also represented the union of Christian and pagan beliefs. A couple of hundred yards from there was *Clochamhóg*, a mass rock, again with two crude crosses cut on its western face. Nearby was a circle of stones on which children had sat to be confirmed when a bishop, on the run, came to meet his people. Everyone knew the 'lookout post' where a man waited to warn of oncoming Redcoats. Penal times seemed recent.

At Donnelly's mill we knew the exact crossing place on Glenalla Burn where Red Hugh, the O'Neill, and the other Ulster chieftains passed for the last time in what we

"We knew exactly where O'Neill and O'Donnell had crossed the Glenalla Burn on their way to exile in 1607."

now know as the Flight of the Earls. The empty bay from where they set sail spoke of dispossession and desertion. The ivy-covered ruins of McSweeney's fort in Rathmullan resounded with broken grandeur and a sense of loss. In Rathmullan too, there is 'the battery', a solid reminder of Britain's attempts to defend herself from Napoleonic invasion. The British connection is deep and long.

The Swilly was a Treaty port. My mother remembered the bay, black with the British fleet. You could walk, she said, from Rathmullan to Buncrana across the decks of battle ships. German U-boats waited at the mouth of the Swilly. Their victims' hulls were sometimes visible at low tide. An American plane crashed on the beach at Portsalon. One of my father's prized possessions was the water flask he salvaged from the wreckage. That wreckage too sometimes emerged from the shifting sands of the Swilly.

In Milford, there was the workhouse and the fever hospital. I drove cattle to the fair of Milford, past the ruins, on the 23rd of every month. In the 1970s, bulldozers were brought in to flatten it and to cart away the stone. As a young teacher I was full of indignant bourgeois outrage, keen to preserve 'our architectural heritage'. My mother took a different view, she said, 'I hope they tumble every stone and flatten that terrible place.' She remembered that three of her family had died there and that her grandmother had walked four miles barefoot, carrying her young son in her arms, to escape. She had no sentimentality about the fine architecture.

At Ray Bridge was the home of the Delaps, our local landlords. I remember the ancient owner, the last of her name, showing me a window with a W cut in the glass. She swore that it was the signature of John Wesley who was said to have stayed overnight on an evangelical tour of Ireland. The house is now in ruins, the glass smashed.

These and a hundred other sites and stories resound in my memory, fill my heart and my head, go with me wherever I go. They're my heart's townland. Everyone has the same bank of precious memory. More precious perhaps, by being unwritten, unmediated by scholarship, a sense of defying the experts with a private lore. An inside track on what really matters and who we really are. In our hearts we know there are no experts. For example, Gortnavern dolmen is, they say, a 'ceremonial site'. What does that mean? The experts don't know who built it, their language, their beliefs, their hopes or their fears, and yet if we listen carefully to 'ordinary' people we can sometimes hear the echo of inherited memory, preserved in a place name, a story, or real knowledge.

I remember once, being on an archaeological field trip in the Sperrins which was led by a very well informed archaeologist. We were at a chambered cairn and we all wondered how our early ancestors had managed to find or shape such impressive rectangular rocks long before the days of diamond tipped blades. We were baffled until one of our number, a local farmer called John Brolly, said that he knew. 'They'd light a huge bonfire around the rock', he said, 'and when the stone was red hot, they got some cold water and poured it in a straight line across the rock. The rock cracked, leaving a perfect straight edge.'

And so for 2000 years the memory of that technique had been preserved from father to son in that valley in the Sperrins. In fact, according to John, it was still being used to shape building stones into his grandfather's time.

Flax bruisers at Ray, photographed by the distinguished Ulster photographer, Robert Welch, in 1893. "I was proud to find that RJ Welch had been paying attention to Ray all those years ago."

The Heart's Townland can be exclusive, wary of outsiders, of their naivety and their disdain. The unwary researcher, or indeed, Ordnance Surveyor, was often told a pack of lies. This outsider child knew instinctively that the narrative of the place was perhaps a way of becoming an insider. Maybe, in retrospect, it was a vain hope.

So much was preserved in anecdote. The narrative explores and presents our shared experience. Society, like individuals, makes sense of experience through telling tales. As Huw Weldon, one of the BBC's great pioneers, said:

> It is through stories, overwhelmingly, that we learn to live in the world: and it is though stories that we learn to live with ourselves. It is no accident that civilisations are built on myths and that religions are built on parables.

Here are some parables from our place. Each concerns a first; the surprise of the new in a very traditional setting:

> Tea first appeared in a station house where the family was keen to offer it to the local priest with his breakfast. After brewing the tea the woman of the house carefully extracted all the tea leaves and served them to the priest on a saucer with a lump of butter in the middle – exactly as she would have served potatoes. The bemused priest asked, 'Would you be good enough mam, to give me a drink of the water that this stuff was boiled in?' People were taken aback by the strange appetites of the clergy!

And then there is the story of the first gun:

> In my time, ours was the last house on the side of a hill before the heather and the rough ground began, but in years gone by, there were more families. McCarrons lived further up above our house. Mary McCarron was the last of her name. One day, when down at the Post Office, she met a young man on leave from the British Army. To impress her he fired his muzzle loader at a passing pigeon. He missed the pigeon, but scared the wits out of Mary who ran home in terror. On passing my grandfather at our gate, she shouted, 'Michael, Michael, how far do you run from you're shot till you fall?'

And the last of the firsts is the arrival of the telephone:

> A young neighbour, a man from Glenvar, the last of our local Gaeltachts, like so many of my neighbours, went away to work in Glasgow. When he was there a couple of years, he decided to put a phone in his mother's house. Every Sunday night at 8.00 he'd ring home for a chat. After a few weeks he said, 'Mammy, why are we speaking English on the phone? When I'm at home we always speak Irish.' His mother said, 'Ah Son, don't be foolish, sure this machine would never understand the Irish.'

The spirit of the townlands was preserved in the narrative – stories that everyone knew. The blood stains on a rock where a land-steward was killed by the tenants. The crow's foot on a ditch left by the sappers and miners of the Ordnance Survey. The townland is a place where all time converges – where the Danes and the Redcoats rub shoulders.

And speaking of time, here's a yarn from the great Ulster folklorist, Michael

J Murphy:

> A yankee came home one time to visit his bachelor cousin. After a night's drinking the American slept soundly until he was woken by the noise of his cousin's feet walking back and forth on the gravel to the garden across the street. Intrigued by the tooing and froing he got up to see the Irishman carrying a wee pig into the garden. Curiosity overcame him so he followed and watched as his cousin held the piglet up to eat a couple of apples from the tree and then bring it back to the sty where he picked up another and repeated the process. After a while he couldn't resist asking, 'Hey wouldn't it be better to put the apples in a pail and bring them to the pigs rather than bringing the pigs one by one to the apples?' 'Why would I do that?' asked his cousin. 'Well,' said the American, 'it would be far less time consuming.' 'Sure, what's time to a pig?' came the retort.

The Heart's Townland isn't just about myth and sentiment - not just the abstract. If you believe, like James Joyce, that Tara is best seen from Holyhead, the exile's eye is particularly keen, uncluttered by recent experience. The exile sees things vividly, recalls every turn on the old bog road, smells the very corn they're cutting in Creeslough. Picture Joyce in Trieste with his street map of Dublin ensuring every shop, every pub and every corner mentioned in *Ulysses* was accurate. Bloom walked on real streets, not fictional ones.

For me, I can see every stone in that cashel wall, every step on the path to the well. I can hear the sound of the mountain burn as it fell from the spout, I can feel the sting of the whitewash on my hand. I can see the beauty of a well-built stack. But nothing's more vivid than smell. The first scent of a whin in bloom and I'm transported back to Ray school - not only seeing what I saw then, but feeling that deep sense of fear and foreboding that filled my every journey to school.

"From the yard of Ray school you looked across at Delap's neat fields."

Those of us who care about these things can trace precisely the march ditch that divides our land from the neighbours. 'That half a rood of rock, a no mans land':

That was the year of the Munich bother. Which

Was more important? I inclined

To lose my faith in Ballyrush and Gortin

Till Homer's ghost came whispering to my mind

He said: I made the Iliad from such

A local row. Gods make their own importance.

Patrick Kavanagh, '*Epic*'

He wasn't Homer, but we too had our poet. His name was Paddy MacSwine. He had no doubt that he was descended from the proud MacSweeneys of Rathmullen Abbey. He was dead long before my time. His house was wall steads, just like the other seven houses in the 'heich toon' - Upper Ray. All are now derelict, the inhabitants dead or gone to America. But Paddy's

Pat Loughrey at the ruins of 'the heich toon', the high town, Upper Ray, 2004.

words survived, printed under his *nom de plume*, 'Amelia A Porter', in very early editions of *Old Moore's Almanac* and *The Irish Gem*. Paddy's poems were puzzles which had to be solved like arithmetic. Most people could make nothing of them, but he was held in high esteem. Poems matter. My mother tried to follow Paddy's rhyming ways. She would have been proud beyond words had she lived to see one of her poems recorded on a video by John Kerr, a modern local hero.

No one described it like Patrick Kavanagh. Who else could see and experience the god of imagination waking in a Mucker fog. All poets and songsters have something in common - they see the wonder and the beauty of the everyday, the ordinary and the unloved. The Heart's Townland is often an act of cultural defiance – someone speaking up, at last, for Inishkeen or Glenalla. As JB Keane said, 'The whole world's in a street in Listowel if you only had the eyes to see it.' Heaney has no doubt of the universal significance of Mossbawn, or Dylan Thomas of the unloved Mumbles, or Ted Hughes of Heptonstall. 'Gods make their own importance.' Like Dylan Thomas, or Robbie Burns, gods recognise that it's not just the story that matters but the language in which it's told.

"All through my childhood the cart waited for a horse – and it's still waiting."

Our dialect in north-east Donegal was a treasure trove reflecting historical experience. The Irish language was, of course, there in the structure of every sentence and in so many words. But hearing us, Catholic and Covenanter alike, speak, outsiders thought we were Scottish. Every wall was a 'waal', every door a 'duur', every cow a 'coo'. And yet there was a layer of old English – a female calf was a 'quay' and 'docken' preserved the ancient plural. What we said, and the way we said it, was evidence in itself of a rich and shared experience.

So what's our role, as Ulster people who feel and know the value of locality? What do we do? Despite the lesson in my mother's attitude to the destruction of the workhouse, do try to prevent the relentless JCB from devouring our landscape. As John Montague said, our fumbling fingers read the braille of our topography and ancient sites to understand those who have gone before us. That braille is being destroyed every day by mechanical diggers. Resist. And, as people who love history, resist those disdainful professional historians who, like some archaeologists, tend to know the measurements of everything but the value of nothing.

We know that sites and places live and breathe through their stories. Yeats warned us against the gombeen men who added pound to greasy pound until they dried the marrow from the bone. Well, there's a certain kind of historiography which adds fact to greasy fact until all feeling's gone. Don't be intimidated by the professionals. Don't be ashamed of sentiment, of your own voice, of your knowledge. Exult in what you've inherited. Then listen and learn.

My father was in the County Hospital in Lifford for the last months of his life. In the final couple of weeks I spent with him, sitting by his bed, he told me practically every yarn he knew. All of them were about the places and the people he loved. That experience made me very conscious that I was a link in a chain. His memory was failing so he'd often forget the end of his stories, and I'd finish them for him. He'd laugh as if he'd never heard them before – delighted, I think, that the stories had been saved, at least for a time. The stories were his gift, more precious than any other inheritance. Maybe the wealth of this lore was more prized because he had so few material things. We listen to these stories, learn and pass them on; the narrative retains the wisdom of generations past. Our last and most significant responsibility is to remember with pride and affection those who've gone before us because we know that 'immortality is conferred by another remembering.'

To conclude I'll tell you one of the yarns he told me in that hospital. My father spent thirty years of his life as a 'Surface man' for Donegal County Council - countless hours darning potholes, cleaning water tables, napping stones and cutting hedges. He never liked the work but had to stick at it because our farm was too small to sustain us. He was a 'ganger' and each summer his little team was supplemented by a few unwilling recruits; small farmers, and the like, who were obliged to take on this work to keep the dole. One man was a notoriously lazy, and on a fine summer's afternoon, as they were working near the Milford workhouse, he lay down on the bank along the roadside and fell sound asleep. The gang left him in peace and at the end of the day slipped away quietly. He didn't stir until he was woken by a woman on her way to a station mass in the Lagg chapel. She shook him, thinking he might have been dead. On waking, he immediately asked the time. 'A quarter past seven', was the response. 'Oh God Almighty,' he said, 'I should have stopped work at half five.'

Sunrise at Ray Bridge, County Donegal.

Townlands: territorial signatures of landholding and identity

Patrick Duffy

A townland down in Monaghan! Ah surely

This makes me glad. I know these names. I can see

The Garlands and the Rooneys and the Quigleys

Neighbours' children in the field next to me

Playing where a bewitched blackthorn's growing

Beside a pile of fairy whinstone rocks

That no man dreams of quarrying - not knowing

What's hid beneath, who here at midnight walks.

I saw it all not far from Tivadina….

Patrick Kavanagh, '*March is a Silversmith*'[1]

My sister, who is a nurse in London, recently visited a hospital in Essex and one of the staff, on discovering that she was from Monaghan, said so was she. My sister responded, 'Well, actually, I'm not from Monaghan town, but from Castleblayney.' To which the other replied, 'I'm from Ballybay.' And my sister said, 'Well I'm not actually from Castleblayney, but a small place outside it called Cremartin.' And the other woman said, 'Well, in fact, I'm not from Ballybay but from Aghnamullen.'

There is a certain territorial logic to our referencing points when we describe where we are from. In the Bronx or Melbourne, or London, there is little point in introducing oneself as being from Ballynahalisk (County Cork), or Drumskinney and Montiaghroe (County Fermanagh).[2] It is obviously a question of scale. But there is also a latent sense of 'It's-such-a-small-rural-backward-blip-on-the-landscape' that I wouldn't mention it. This was especially true up to forty or fifty years ago, when there was a sensitivity about rural rusticity, reflected in the term 'culchie'. Until the 1960s, for example, there was a notable gap in living standards and lifestyles between rural and urban throughout the country. The rural townlands had no electricity, for instance, and with that came a big difference in living conditions. My mother and her generation lived in houses with oil lamps, candles, and pot ovens; where as a girl she ironed her school uniform with an old smoothing iron and dried her hair at the fireside; where she and the other 'country girls' were regularly identified as being different in the St Louis school in Monaghan town. Thus our emigrants airbrushed these townland places from their identities when they moved away. Now, of course, living standards have converged, and

Townland boundary markers in County Mayo (left) and County Armagh.

there is a new self-conscious pride in the distinctive names and local heritage of the townlands, reflected in the manner in which many of them in different parts of Ireland have their names carved on roadside stone markers.

Patrick Kavanagh, who could in many ways be described as the first poet of the townlands, regularly invoked their names in his writing. Although sometimes he had his doubts, as when he says in 'Epic': 'I inclined to lose my faith in Ballyrush or Gortin…' until Homer's ghost assured him how important such local places were. Seamus Heaney in a preface to the Federation for Ulster Local Studies publication, *Every Stoney acre has a name*, summarised his own personal discovery of the centrality of meaning of townland for a young fellow coming in from the rural margins, who felt 'the fume of affection and recognition' that came off the word when he saw it written down on official paper in a book in his local library. (It was in John Hewitt's poem 'The Townland of Peace'.) Heaney saw it as an affirmation of the importance of townland and, a bit like Kavanagh with Homer, 'a premonition of demarginalization' passed over him.[3]

Clearly townlands have enormous social, cultural and psychological importance for rural people in Ireland. For those of us from rural places, we take this for granted. For example, they are a fundamental part of our 'activity space' - the place we know best, where we move up and down, back and forth, every day; where the topographies of place and people are best known; where, for those born into townlands, first memories are rooted and never really forgotten. In the following discussion, I will examine the significance of townland for identity and belonging.

Since the townland is so important for identity, it is obviously also important when we come to understand the past. It becomes a kind of lens through which we can see the past experienced in our local landscapes. Therefore I will look at the townland as a resource for historians, especially local historians, in examining the past in local places, and how it emerged as an important local unit for farming and landholding. Indeed the whole material fabric of the landscape which has been principally generated by farming and its activities took place predominantly within the framework of townlands.

Signatures carry notions of identity, individual character, personality, and thus might appropriately express the way these small territorial units have been inscribed on the rural (and urban) landscape. Townlands are local places which have distinctive characteristics like shape and size, location, names, identity, personality or sense of place. They each have histories, constructed and remembered by their inhabitants, which mesh together to form patterns of regional geography and history.

Townlands, therefore, can be summarised as follows:

- They comprise territories, with shape, size and physical features often reflected in boundaries and shape. Maps of townland networks show them as a lattice of lines and spaces intimately bound up with the topography of the landscape. Apart from variations in size throughout the country, shape and boundaries reflect the historical experience of landscape: in Ulster generally townland boundaries flow with the land, following streams and brooks; in Kildare and other Pale counties, boundaries are more angular, reflecting a greater amount of intervention and moulding by local populations in the past.

- Townlands are extremely local, survivals of a more local world in the past, so that when we travel far away (and up the urban hierarchy) they go out of focus. That they remain a part of people's identity is manifested in the numbers of houses in Dublin, and other cities and towns in Ireland and elsewhere, which are named after such distant and remembered local places - 'the heart's townland'?

- What might be called 'agents of localisation' operate through the lattice of townland spaces and names. Placenames, like surnames and personal

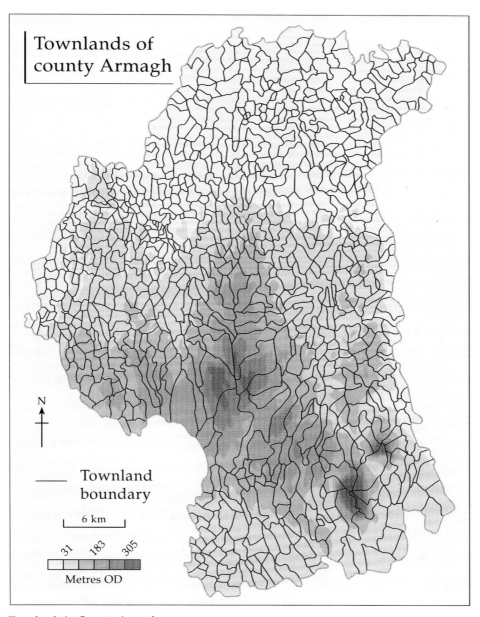

Townlands of county Armagh

N

—— Townland boundary

6 km

31 183 305

Metres OD

Townlands in County Armagh.
(*From:* Atlas of the Irish rural landscape, *Cork 1997*)

names, are very strong markers of identity and belonging. As postal addresses they are labels of locality with families being identified with townlands: the Kellys of Blackhall, the McCabes of Shancoduff. Family name associations with townlands are repeated again and again in all studies, and by anyone who knows anything about rural Ireland. Surname concentrations in different parts of Ireland are a broader reflection of the local townland significance of people and place.[4] Even though postal workers operate over more extensive districts now from delivery vans, not bicycles as in the past, the townlands are still vital links between national and local. Current proposals in the Republic of Ireland to close more local post offices, and to install postboxes for easier delivery have drawn a lot of fire from local communities. The Post Office's decision in Northern Ireland over thirty years ago to replace townland addresses with road names and house numbers has caused major controversy in rural areas there. Townland addresses are powerfully embedded in local consciousness.

- Churches also operated through the townland and parish network. A generation and more ago the Catholic church (and other churches, as Jack Johnston shows in this volume) had a wide range of services, not only on Sundays, but on evenings and weekdays, when lists of family and townland names were regularly invoked for a variety of community purposes – and the (mis)pronunciation of townland names by visiting clergy always identified them as outsiders! Similarly, the Catholic Church in many parts of the country operated a network of 'station masses' which mirrored the townland network, with townland households being involved in an annual cyclical hosting of church services.

- The network of townlands fitted into the more pedestrian local world up to the 1950s and 60s, when people cycled or walked, or plodded on horse cart through the landscape. The local geography of townland matched such a local scale of movement: my father's daily journey from school where he taught was by bike in the 1930s, and in summer he regularly called into houses, or met and talked with people on the road. Nowadays cars sweep past and have little connection with the texture of this local world.[5]

- Farmers' lives and farm work take place within the townland. In the past, harvest teamwork, *meithealls*, neighbours swapping and joining their labour, and the seasonal and daily grind of ploughing, or harrowing and haymaking, made the townland and its fields and local features intimately known and named. Farms were clearly identified with townlands. This is the ultimate defining feature of the townland because, as historians know, the townland was, and continues to be, intimately connected with landholding and landownership. It was the ultimate territorial mechanism through which farms and leases and agricultural activity were organised for some hundreds of years. Even though farming is not as important as it was, the townland is the greatest legacy of our history of farms and land

- and the boundaries of holdings which make up farms today reflect this older significance of townland boundaries for farm structure.   Indeed settlement patterns, both today and in the past, were forged in the moulds of the townlands.   Historically, for different parts of the island, they provide an explanatory context for settlement features such as the farm cluster, the dispersed pattern of farmsteads, the 'townland farm' with its ribbon of cottages on the perimeter of the townland, the nucleated village, or the 'Big House' of the landowner presiding over his parkland and townland. Today also, rural renewal of landscapes and commuter settlements echo faintly the more ancient topologies of townlands.

Although the townland is important in many ways, it must be conceded that as the life of the Irish countryside is changing, as more people live in towns or commute to towns, there is declining connection with the land, and knowledge of townlands and their contents is also perhaps fading.   A couple of decades ago, the editor of this volume, Brian Turner, undertook a little experiment with three generations of men of similar background in the same parish of rural County Down which illustrated a contraction in knowledge of local topographies.   The oldest man, aged 73, could name and place over 150 townlands and his mental map of his locality was one where people and places, townlands and farms were meshed closely together.   A younger farmer in his forties was able to name thirteen townlands, and his sixteen-year-old son was sure only of the identity of the townland in which he lived.[6] Although this reflects the particular impact of the 'official' introduction of road names in place of townland addresses in Northern Ireland, it is a pattern of change that is also reflected in loss of memory of field and other micro names within townlands and their farms.[7]   Farmers and farm families who traditionally worked in the fields day in and day out, up and down the headlands, up and down the roads, meeting neighbours constantly, knew the townlands and their inhabitants.   Now farm numbers are falling. Perhaps farmers on tractors have different relationships with fields, farms and townlands, and non-farm newcomers often have even more limited local connections.   So therefore these markers of locality and the local are possibly fading from local memory and knowledge? It is no coincidence that it is at such a crucial juncture that conferences such as 'The heart's townland: marking boundaries in Ulster', are convened to celebrate or highlight the townland when it may be in process of fading from collective consciousness.

Genealogy and geometry of townlands

Much work on the historical significance of townlands in Ireland has been undertaken in the North.   It may be that the threat of obliteration of the townland network by the Post Office in the early seventies raised public consciousness of this valuable heritage.   Tom McErlean's 1983 paper on townlands in Ireland was an important attempt to seek out and highlight an island-wide pattern in townland and other territorial units in Ireland. More recent case studies of townlands have been important also in demonstrating methodologies for studying the historical development and significance of townlands.[8] Mainstream historians have generally devoted little attention to the roots of the townland system.[9] Geographical information systems (GIS) and computerised databases are also facilitating greater use of the matrix of townlands and townland-based historical information.[10]

There are about 62,000 townland units in Ireland as recorded by the Ordnance Survey in the 1830s. A great many in marginal and mountain areas have been abandoned or planted in forestry - in Leitrim and Fermanagh for instance. In these kinds of places, there is little doubt that the townlands will be lost and forgotten. Nevertheless it is possible with the assistance of GIS technology to examine social and demographic changes today and in the past through the framework of the townland. Townland populations and numbers of houses are published for every census from 1841 until 1911. And such information is increasingly accessible for more recent times as well, so that townlands continue to be an important analytical tool for local studies. Donegal County Council has recently produced an atlas, for example, which presents a range of census data such as population change and household numbers by townland for 1996.[11] It also shows extensive swathes of the county which are uninhabited.

Many of the poorer marginal districts in Ireland may only have been divided into named townlands relatively late, from the seventeenth century, as population expanded into them. In Ulster, some of the restrictions on Gaelic Irish settlement during the Plantation period may have pushed people into these areas. There was a noteworthy degree of local mobility of population between neighbouring townland units in the seventeenth century, as evidenced in the Hearth Money Rolls.[12] But most were inhabited and even those not inhabited several centuries ago were still named, often in association with lowland townlands. Farmland, mountain commonage, summer uplands and turbary were all linked in a network of economic and social interrelationships.[13]

If one compares a square kilometre in Ireland with other parts of Europe, one will note that Ireland is exceptional in having this unique array of very small local territorial divisions. However, 'uniqueness' can be an obstacle to understanding for historians: most things are connected and valuable lessons can be drawn from comparative studies. Ireland's apparently unique legacy of townland places seems to be a fortuitous by-product of the country's particular experience of land and landscape in the sixteenth and seventeenth centuries. The survival of our intricate network of townlands is essentially a legacy of what might be called a colonial past.

Most rural parts of Europe also had a similar process of territorialisation, or dividing up the land into a range of smaller territorial entities, as exemplified by the 'toun' in Scotland or the 'tref' in Wales. It was associated with land assessment, stocking capacity, local forms of taxes and renders in lordships and chiefries. The *tricha cét* or hundred appears to have been a characteristic land division across Europe, with a vertical range of diminishing subdivisions underneath. In Ireland, the ploughlands (*seisreach* in Irish) seem to have had English or Scottish equivalents. From such a superstructure, our modern townland sprang. The townships of the Scottish islands and highlands were very similar and lasted into the eighteenth century, to fall into decline following the clearances and radical upheavals of farming communities.[14] All the smaller local entities seem to have evolved into obscurity in most other parts of northern Europe.

Thus, in common with the rest of these islands, Gaelic Ireland had a highly spatialised landscape assessment system, expressed in a territorial hierarchy of large and small units whose boundaries were held in local memories. It might be thought of as a system which emerged from the bottom up, at local level, and which was used from top down by lords and chief landholding families for allocating the burdens of cesses and dues on their kinsfolk.[15] In parts of the country there are early records of this territorial system in twelfth-century listings of names and places. McNeill has demonstrated the existence of many of the modern townlands in Down at the end of the early Christian period, for example.[16] Papal correspondence with Clogher diocese contains references to these units in the early fourteenth century, which might repay further investigation.[17] Ó Buachalla has charted the development of the complete list of townlands in the Fermoy area from *Crichad an Chaoilli* in the Book of Lismore from the twelfth and early thirteenth centuries.[18] The coincidence of parishes, established in the twelfth century, with ballybetaghs in Monaghan and other parts of Ulster suggests that the internal subdivisions of these ballybetaghs were fairly intact as early as the twelfth century.[19]

The Elizabethan administration in Ireland set out to try to record and map this territorial system, as part of a process of regulating the distribution of lands among the Gaelic lords in Monaghan, and of organising new immigrant settlers in the plantation schemes in other parts of Ulster. Inquisitions were held throughout the counties to establish the boundaries and names of owners and the resultant geometry of units is represented, for instance, in some of Josias Bodley's largely impressionistic maps for the Ulster plantation counties and in the lists of the 1591 divisions of lands for Monaghan.[20]

Ireland and Europe of five centuries ago was a very local, essentially pre-modern world, with cultural traditions and customs, for instance, such as measures and weights, distance and area, being particular to localities or local lordships. Although they had locally specific names, a geometry of fractions of land was characteristic across Ireland as a whole, reflecting in many cases arrays of local assessments of stocking or cropping capacity.

Names for territorial units in Ireland in the sixteenth century (after T McErlean, 1983).

In Donegal, Tyrone and Coleraine, for instance, there were ballybetaghs - *Baile biataigh* - subdivided into ballyboes - *Baile bó*. Quarters comprised one quarter of a ballybetagh, referred to in some places by four smaller named units, as in the ballybetagh of Strabane, for example, where there is a reference to 'Leck, being halfe a quarter containing two Ballibose'.[21] In Monaghan and Fermanagh the tate was the equivalent of the ballyboe of neighbouring territories. Gneeves, pottles and pints (using liquid measures as a form of land evaluation) were smaller assessment systems very similar to the pennylands, ouncelands and merklands of the Scottish highlands. They were measures of stocking capacity or land value which could be translated into local renders to the lord. In general, in many parts of the north and west of the country, the ballybetagh emerges as a primary territorial unit, with a fairly regular subdivision from quarters to sixteenths. In subsequent seventeenth-century developments in landholding, the ballybetagh fell out of usage and the more flexible smaller units endured as building blocks of property to emerge by the late seventeenth century throughout Ireland as townlands.

This emerging geometry of territorial units provided a framework for landholding, with kin groups slotted into an architecture of tates or ballyboes (or equivalents such as polls in other areas), quarters and ballybetaghs.[22] In Farney in south Monaghan in 1612, five ballybetaghs (of eighty tates) were divided among nineteen tenants, all of 'these being of one sept,' resembling the tacksmen discussed by Dodgshon for Kintyre and Harris, where kinsmen of the chief held the land in clusters of townships under whom numbers of subtenants worked.[23] In the 1591 division of the lands of Monaghan, the ballybetaghs of Balledrumgowla and Ballymcgowne showed clear evidence of kin relations in the names of their freeholder tenants, McHugh Roe McMahons, McShane McMahons and McBreine McMahons being most common. In Balleglaslagh, two tates each were held by Patrick McCabe, Arte Boy McQuaide, Tege McQuaide, Nele oge McQuaide, Patrick McGillegrome McQuaid, Rosse McMahon McPatrick and Melaghlin McMahon. Patrick McQuaid McPhelym and Art McQuaid both held one tate each, making a grand total of sixteen tates, mostly held by McQuaids. The ballybetagh of Balleglanka (in present-day Castleshane) consisted of sixteen tates held mostly by O'Clerians. In all cases the tates were individually named and are identifiable with townlands today.[24] It is likely that these small divisions existed as a territorial structure independent of demographic factors. Many tates in Monaghan and Farney in the early seventeenth century, for instance, were composed of untenanted grazing lands, held by larger 'gentlemen' farmers, as a Farney survey called them. If and when population increased, these units could be more intensively farmed as the need arose. Tates were amalgamated into groups of two, three or more and held by a freeholder tenant. As more tenant kin became available, they could be broken up again. In the barony of Trough in the north of Monaghan county, and in other lordships in the west of the country, these small units were even fragmented into halves, as with half tates in Monaghan.

In other areas, many townlands which emerged into the light of day (through the maps and records of the seventeenth century) had earlier been subsumed in larger quarters, which may have contained up to four smaller units: John Cunningham's study of Drumskinney and Montiaghroe in Fermanagh suggests such a process.[25] Sandra Millsopp's case study of Bangor refers to the Five Quarters, which disappeared from local usage early on, with one quarter continuing as a townland.[26] In Clontibret parish in Monaghan, there is an area still known locally as the Black Quarter, which refers back to a portion of the original ballybetagh, and which loosely refers to four townlands. Quarters were much more common divisions in Connacht and it was mainly these which translated into modern townlands in the west of the country.

In the Pale counties of Meath and Kildare, ploughlands, or plowlands (and half ploughlands), were the units of assessment which may have roughly approximated to the townland.[27] Any pre-Norman hierachy of territorial units appears to have been subsumed into a structure of ploughlands within manors. *Seisreach* was the Gaelic equivalent of ploughland, and was reckoned by John O'Donovan to be the equivalent of a quarter of a ballybetagh.[28] Many of the records of manorial Ireland from the late medieval period up to the mid-seventeenth century surveys also refer to 'town and lands' separately from ploughlands (also called carucates in earlier records). Ploughlands continued as a local rural measure of land assessment up to the nineteenth century in Kildare, though the Civil Survey referred to 'towne and lands' in its tabular data.

The usage of 'townland' would appear to have been part of a gradual transition to standardisation by administrators who were dealing centrally with these recurring territorial entities, which appeared to share common patterns and antecedents but had different local nomenclatures. In some of the counties in the Civil Survey, such as in the new county of Londonderry, 'towne lands' are used for land denominations. Inquisitions in 1626 to do with the Ulster Plantation referred to 'townlands' in the barony of Strabane, though in the Civil Survey ballyboes are the units used.[29]

It is difficult, therefore, to summarise what we might characterise as the genealogical origins of townland. By the sixteenth and seventeenth centuries it had a convoluted evolution from a mishmash of local regional territorial denominations, in a range of Gaelic and feudal manorial lordships, in a variety of termon and church lands, other monastic lands, and far-flung Gaelic territories which may have had some superficial cultural similarity but had developed largely independent of each other. In other words, here was a medieval world where political and social authority was regionally fragmented. Only with the arrival of 'modernising' tendencies, in our case the British state with its administrative bureaucracy, did central authority emerge to consolidate these fragmented margins into a unified entity.

Monaghan is a good case study because it has a fairly clear record in 1591 and subsequently. Airghialla was one of several Gaelic territories in south Ulster which was 'shired' as county Monaghan in 1575. It had internally distinctive experiences of landholding and lordship, but there were patterns of similarity with other parts of Gaelic Ireland in the geometry of their territorial structures, in terms of fractions of a quarter, half and sixteenths of a ballybetagh - a range of small and very small local territorialisations.

The problem for historians, scholars (and English administrators at the time) has been that a great many of the units and names were measures of assessment rather than area, reflecting the capacity of a place to produce the 'the grass of so many cows' or 'so much corn' rather than a definite number of acres. They did, of course, have boundaries, which could be recited and mapped. The confusion has perhaps arisen from attempts to assume a standard acreage equivalent to these units. Elizabethan records showed the ploughland acreages as follows: 'Meath about 600 acres; in Louth about 300 acres; in the County of Dublin about 200; in Kildare about 200 acres.'[30] This kind of irregularity irritated civil servants and revenue gatherers who wanted some kind of equitable taxation scheme and often went for a standard quotient of 60 or 120 acres of arable land, which caused many problems in setting up estates during the plantations. In retrospect, it was futile for the colonial administration in the sixteenth and seventeenth centuries to seek a standard acreage. These attempts at translation, usually referring to 'arable' with the acreage of waste excluded, hinted at the economic reality behind the old assessment system. McErlean has summarised it well:

> ... area measurement is of limited value as an index of agricultural worth. An acre of bog, for instance, is not equal in value to one of arable. An estimate of the content of each land type such as arable, pasture, meadow, turbary and wood provides the basis for an accurate evaluation of land potential. It is certain that the assessment systems took this into consideration. [31]

What we can say, therefore, is that out of this *pot pourri* of units, the modern state in the seventeenth century, and its associated new landowning estate system, forged a more homogeneous and universal standard of territorial structure which eventually came to be called a townland. Because of their regionally specific historical roots, it is probably pointless to seek an average national profile of a townland. The variety of townland sizes reflects not only development within separate medieval territories, but also variable expressions of land assessment and agricultural potential and diversity in the physical landscape. There is, therefore, an evident environmental logic in the geography of townlands. Broadly speaking, townlands appear to be smaller in the better lands, for instance in north Armagh and neighbouring parts of Monaghan, and much larger in the hill and mountain uplands of south Armagh and the parish of Aghnamullen in south Monaghan. Townlands average 104 and 135 acres respectively in Tehallen and Donagh parishes of north Monaghan; 255 and 276 acres in the hillier and poorer lands of Aghnamullen and Muckno parishes. In the hill country of Newtownhamilton and Creggan parishes in south Armagh they average 563 and 376 acres respectively. McErlean points out that townland size throughout the island may also be related to the size of the original Gaelic lordships, with smaller lordships tending to have more fragmentation and subdivision of their ballybetaghs to accommodate population pressure.

In the south Ulster drumlin belt one can also see an environmental logic in the relationship between the townland net and landscape topography. Townlands normally contain drumlin cores, often with hill-top raths or ringforts reflecting dry-point settlements from the early medieval period. Boundaries run through the wet, marshy, intervening bottom lands, following the small streams which characterise the impeded drainage of the drumlin region. Four centuries of husbandry and improvement have reclaimed much of the marshy wetlands, which contemporary documents transcribed from Irish usage as 'curraghs.' In Thomas Raven's 1634 survey of the Essex estate in south Monaghan, boglands and lakes always fell on the boundaries of the tates.[32] The geography of field patterns within the townlands in the drumlin country also often follows the shape and topography of townlands. It is possible in many instances to discern primary field boundaries and leading fences superimposed along the spine of drumlins, which have later subdivided fields to accommodate growing populations.

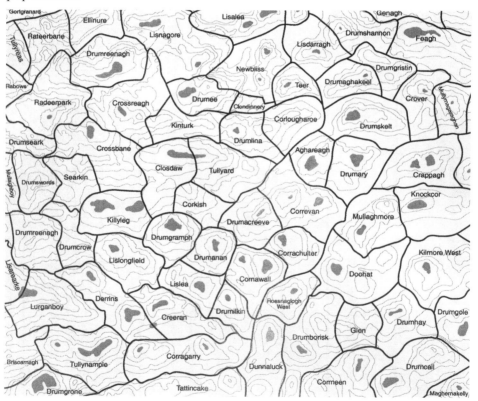

Townlands and topography in west Monaghan, hilltops shaded.

Contemporary descriptions of boundaries of townland units (as incorporated in parish boundaries) are important because such verbal records of boundaries show the manner in which they followed existing permanent features in the physical landscape, such as streams or mountain features.   In the barony of Strabane, the Civil Survey describes the bounds of the manor of Downelonge (consisting of thirty-two ballyboes or two former ballybetaghs):

> … from the top of the mountain [named Cullen] it goeth southeastward, to the head of a bogg name Oskekoran which bogg is the meare between the said lands and the Churchlands of the said parish untell it fall into a brooke name Ishland which brooke is another meare between the said lands until it fall into Dennett water, and upwards by this water untell itt cometh neere under the olde Castle of Downemanagh, where it leaveth the water and goeth southwestside, thereof streight upp a stone ditch till it come to the foote of the Mountayne from which it goeth streight upwards to the topp of Laate Mountain from which it desendeth by a green sward, to a rise of a little waterbrooke …[33]

Part of the parish of Ardstraw's boundaries repeat this pattern:

> … from thence to ye brooke of Dusertragh, thence downewards to a stone ditch on ye other side of ye brooke, thence to ye forde of Bellinamallogh, thence by a gutter to ye Mountayne glennmc wch devideth betwixt ye lands of Sr. Wm Hamilton in ye parrish of Bodony and ye lands of Sr Wm Stewart in this parrish, wch meares bounds it on ye East, from thence by a litle stream of water wch runeth into ye brooke of Altochall wch brooke…runneth into ye Ushanogh water …[34]

While there are references to stone ditches, which are presumably man-made, it is mostly rivers and streams, bogs, fords, or other permanent landmarks such as large stones or rocks, which demarcate the boundaries, as in the parish of Errigal Keeroge:

> … by the river Blackwater, … thence runs along the river Ballimaken … from thence to Grangegh, … by a brooke called Owen O Quiggerie, from thence westward … to brooke of Glanegarragh and from thence runs along to brooke called Ruckan …[35]

We can assume that the territorial order of baronies, parishes and interlocking townland units have endured fairly tenaciously down through the last millennium. One of the characteristics of boundaries in the landscape is that when they acquire a social, cultural or economic significance (as with landholding properties or estates such as ballybetaghs or churchlands or termons) there is an inbuilt inertia in their location which makes them remembered and lasting. And all other modifications to the landscape such as settlement, housing, fields and farms and fences, drainage and the general 'improvements' of the eighteenth and nineteenth centuries, occur within the stable network of these pre-existing territorial units.

Names

Seamus Heaney, John Hewitt, Patrick Kavanagh, and John Montague, to name four poets of Ulster, have regularly invoked the names of these little local distinctive places lying at the heart of community.   They have identified with the musical rhythm in lists of townland names, like Hewitt's 'Drumbo,

Dungannon or Annalong'. Even the first few townlands in the parish of Iniskeen in south Monaghan have a ring to them: Aghaglass, Annagerril, Aughrim Beg, Aughrim More, Ballakelly, Ballintra, Ballyrush and Blackstaff. Local song writers, balladeers and musicians, for generations signifiers of vibrant local identification with place, have mentioned townland names by the score: 'The cliffs of Dooneen', 'The rocks of Bawn', 'The boys of Carrigallen', 'Slieve Gallen brae'.[36]

It is a fundamental part of human instinct to name places, to put the stamp of our community and culture on the landscapes we inhabit and own. Townland names (as well as field names, and to a lesser extent street names) are especially significant local signatures inscribed on the landscape, incorporating in most cases our former native language or regional dialect. The critical event in the history of placenames in Ireland was the seventeenth-century consolidation of its land and landscape in the modern (British) state, accompanied by an extensive array of maps and legal records. Naming practices by local communities from three hundred to one thousand years ago were probably constantly evolving and being modified until they were finally recorded and 'fixed' in documents, land grants, confiscations, surveys, maps, wills, indentures, assignments, and other transactions from the sixteenth century onwards. The townland names continued to evolve down to the nineteenth century in local usage, many becoming corrupted as the Irish language faded. It was in the 1830s, as Myrtle Hill writes elsewhere in this volume, that John O'Donovan and the Ordnance Survey embarked on a last big enterprise, imposing standard anglicised forms on the pronunciation and spelling of the placenames, a process about which O'Donovan expressed himself somewhat diffident. His remarks from Fermanagh in 1834, on the unfavourable reaction of locals to new spellings of their townland names, support today's contentions about the deep-rooted identities embedded in the names, as well as prefiguring the controversy generated by the later cavalier disregard of these placenames by the Post Office, aided by local authorities, in the North.[37]

While this article is not concerned with linguistics it is obviously useful to know what names mean, and to try to understand what gave rise to them. In general one could say that the Gaelic Irish names usually tend to be descriptive of local environmental or topographical conditions in the past, and indeed today, such as names incorporating references to the hilly landscapes of the drumlins, as in *Druim, Cnoc, Cabhán, Tulach, Lurga, Mullach, Ros, Tón*; or the quality of land, like *Eanach, Cluain, Móin*. There is also a numerous range of names which refer to human settlement of the landscape, such as *Lios, Rath, Gort, Achadh, Baile, Dún, Carn* and *Leacht*.

The significance of townland names in English is often overlooked, possibly because it is assumed that Irish names are more 'authentic', and certainly more exotic, in a largely English-speaking society. Townland names in English, concentrated in the Pale regions, have an antiquity as well, often telling a story of active settlement, colonisation and environmental change for hundreds of years. Burntfurze (two each in Kildare and Kilkenny), Blackditch (ten instances, mostly in Kildare and Meath), Blacktrench in Kildare, Redbog (six in Louth, Meath, Kildare, and Kilkenny) reflect the process of reclamation of the land in the middle ages. The Kildare Civil Survey recorded the townlands of Thornberry, Thornhill, Furryhill.   The numbers of Moortowns throughout the Pale represent in most cases reclaimed marsh or bogland.   Blackwood, Shortwood, Allenwood, Broadleas, Whiteleas, Wheatfields, Newland, Loughtown, Kingsfurze, Kingsbog, Ironhills all contain land use references. Newhaggard (four in Meath and Dublin), Pollardstown (in Kildare in 1331), Bleachyard (Mayo), Bleachgreen (two in Kilkenny and Sligo), Bleachlawn (Westmeath) refer to occupation and settlement of the land: curiously the extensive linen industry of Ulster failed to displace older Gaelic townland names.   Although the Irish townland names sometimes incorporate family names, many pre-date modern surnames or the names do not transfer well into the 'Englished' renditions, as reflected possibly in Maghernakelly, Tanmacanally, Tullycumasky, Tonyfinnagan in County Monaghan.   Ó Ceallaigh refers to numerous townlands which incorporate family names in Ulster: Ballyquin, Ballyfatten near Urney (which refers to Pattons), Tamneymullan (near Maghera, referring to O'Mullans - *Uí Mhaoláin*.[38] English and Welsh family names are common in townlands of the Pale, many dating from the fourteenth century and long since faded from local memory: Punchestown, Blanchardstown, Nicholastown, Sherlockstown, Jenkinstown, Guidenstown, Gormanstown, Tankardstown.

Townland geographies are ultimately imprints in the landscape determined by past interlinkages of land, population, settlement and tenants. Why did they endure? Mainly because of the unique interaction of 'agrarian capitalism' as reflected in landed estates and accompanying estate management. Townlands became the templates within which estates managed to improve and modernise their landscape through the agency of the tenant populations associated with the townlands. The new emphasis on commercial rents and market economics which came with the modern state in the seventeenth century meant that estate properties and their territorial subdivisions survived by record. Property assets had to be protected, managed for profit, and handed on. Lands were leased, rented, regulated and recorded for posterity in lists of townland and family names. Griffith's printed mid-nineteenth century valuation is one of the most comprehensive information databases of any European country, with the townlands and their tenant farmers at its core.[39]   There was an enormous regional and local variation in the way estates were directly involved in the nuts and bolts of landscape change and 'improvement'. Some estates, like the Marquis of Downshire's, maintained a great deal of interest in the details of housing, holdings, enclosure and drainage, while others left much of the internal arrangement of townlandscapes to the tenants. In general, estates like that of Kenmare in Kerry, or of Bath, Farnham or Shirley in south Ulster, were interested in the way tidy and orderly landscapes reflected a tidy and orderly tenantry.[40] In many west of Ireland townlands in the post-famine period, landowners and state agencies like the Congested Districts Board were directly involved in squaring fields and re-arranging rural housing accompanied in many instances by assisted migration.

While one can provide neutral descriptions of the central role of townlands in estates, R J Scally has attempted to subvert this by highlighting their contested nature, especially in the west of Ireland, in the nineteenth century.[41] He has observed the manner in which their apparent disorder - represented in complexities of lanes, houses, townland names, fieldnames and nicknames - was exploited by their occupants to confuse, baffle and resist the impositions of 'official' order on the landscape and society of the townlands.

Using combinations of the Valuation lists, the Ordnance Survey, censuses of population and local field work it is possible to see the way in which townlands formed a territorial context for the waxing and waning of population and settlement patterns at the local level. The landed estates in the sixteenth and seventeenth centuries essentially represented bundles of these small units. From being vehicles for the transfer of ownership, townlands subsequently became mechanisms through which the management of estates functioned. This could have all kinds of long-term side effects. For example, the leasing by estates of whole townlands to new settlers resulted in ethnic sorting processes occurring from the beginning: thus swathes of townlands around Newbliss on the Ker estate in west Monaghan, for instance, were 'Protestant' townlands, cheek by jowl with 'Catholic' townlands. In Clontibret parish, the Scotch Corner is located in the midst of 'Presbyterian' townlands. This ethnic checkerboard pattern was repeated in many parts of Ulster, and surfaced as sectarian rural landscapes from early in the nineteenth century, which transferred into the urban townlands along, for example, the Shankill-Falls divide in Belfast.[42]

Estate policies and practices relating to leasing, subdivision of holdings, and subletting to cottiers were inscribed in the landscape of townlands, and these processes invariably occurred with surnames also being mapped onto the townlandscapes. Often today residues of such earlier contrasts in practice from one estate to another echo in the landscapes of modern townlands.

The accompanying map of Tonagh shows the association between farms and houses in one townland in Monaghan, with the inevitable clearing out of farms and houses since the mid-nineteenth century. With consolidation of farm holdings came declining family linkages to townlands. But in spite of such changes the link between the family names and the land of the townland still persists in many places. Narratives of farm holding changes throughout the twentieth century still reflect the outlines of townlands, sifting out the Brannigans and Woods and Kerrs of Annagh, the Carraghers of Mulladuff, the Hughes and Morgans of Annaglogh (in County Monaghan) and so on. This persistence of family, kin, and townland networks was bolstered by localised marriage patterns until a couple of generations ago. As noted earlier, the townland represented a very local world, where movement and interaction was inward-looking, reflected, for instance, in house dances and other forms of socialisation organised almost exclusively on townland lines. Some Sundays

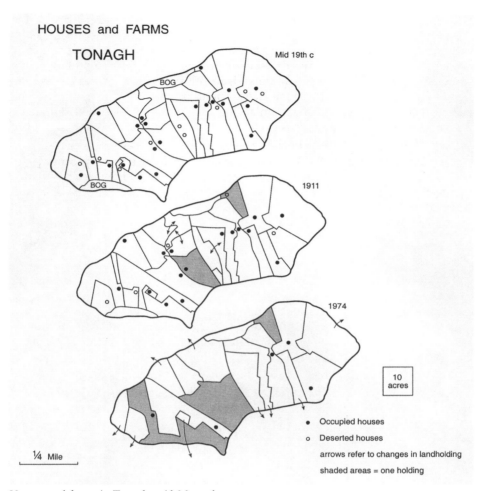

Houses and farms in Tonagh, mid-Monaghan.

in the early twentieth century saw a choice of four or five kitchen dances within a two-mile radius.   In my grandfather's generation, in the opening decades of the twentieth century, marriage 'fields' in rural Monaghan were determined to a great extent by the townland geography.   Thirty-two marriages contracted between 1911 and 1930 in three townlands in a corner of Clontibret parish were highly concentrated, most of the marriages linking several contiguous townlands.   The years after the second world war especially, saw a speeding up of change and a compression of distance which eroded the localness of townland worlds, together with emigration or increasing social isolation, accompanied by increasing mobility as cars were acquired.   And a new picture has emerged in recent decades as many former holdings in the townlands have provided a template for a population renewal as new houses are peppered across the landscape.

The townlandscape of Northern Ireland was subjected to major upheaval in the early 1970s with the Post Office's attempted obliteration of this legacy and its replacement with rural road names which angered so many people across all communities. Of the twenty-six local authorities in Northern Ireland, only Fermanagh had the confidence to reject the road-naming system which so clearly damaged a valued cultural inheritance. Some of the anger, dismay and depth of feeling is captured in the following local reaction soon after the change was implemented:

> Roads are now to be given arbitrary names by faceless officials, who attach arbitrary numbers to them. For example, the old Corbally road [in Dromore parish], according to the Post Office, is to be known as 'St Dympna's Road' on the specious argument that St Dympna's Catholic Church is situated near it. But St Dympna herself never stood on this road, and those who do not attend this church must feel at least nonplussed at this arbitrary action. Those who know the value of these ancient names as badges of personal identification will continue to use them, because they have served our people well for so long, and any change now will surely baffle those who come after us.[43]

The Townlands Campaign in Northern Ireland, fostered by the Federation for Ulster Local Studies, has been focussed on the singular objective of saving townland usage and identity from being lost. This concern may have diverted some attention away from studies of our historical townland legacy and its great significance, to focus more on the nature of the loss and how it can be resisted, a problem which is not yet an issue for the rest of Ireland. However, it should be noted that the fate of the townland at the hands of a modern bureaucracy in the North may very well contain lessons for the future in the Republic of Ireland.

Townlands remain as important places, distinctive local contexts within which the history of landscape and people can be studied, and within which the human need for belonging and community can be expressed in Ireland, north and south.

Notes and references

1 From Peter Kavanagh (ed.), *The complete poems of Patrick Kavanagh* ((New York 1972).
2 These particular townlands are examined in Brian Ó Dálaigh, Denis A Cronin & Paul Connell (eds.) *Irish townlands* (Dublin 1998), and W H Crawford and R H Foy (eds.), *Townlands in Ulster* (Belfast 1998).
3 Seamus Heaney, 'Preface' to Tony Canavan (ed.), *Every stoney acre has a name: a celebration of the townland in Ulster* (Belfast 1991), p xi.
4 For discussion of such localized name concentrations see Brian S Turner, 'Notes on family names in Lecale' in *Lecale Review*, 2003, pp5-14.
5 See P Duffy, 'Change and renewal in issues of place, identity and the local' in Jim Hourihane (ed), *Engaging spaces: people, place and space from an Irish perspective* (Dublin, 2003), pp13-29.
6 Brian Turner, communication, 9-2-02. See also Brian S Turner, 'Mick Taggart's

Townlands', in *Lecale Review*, 2004, forthcoming.

7 P Duffy, 'Unwritten landscapes: reflections on minor placenames and sense of place in the Irish countryside', in H Clarke, M Hennessy, J Prunty (eds.), *Surveying Ireland's past* (Dublin 2004).

8 T McErlean, 'The Irish townland system of landscape organisation' in T Reeves-Smyth and F Hamond (eds.), *Landscape archaeology of Ireland* (Oxford 1983); Ó Dalaigh, *Irish townlands*; Crawford and Foy, *Townlands in Ulster.*; see also Angelique Day and Patrick McWilliams (eds.), *Ordnance Survey Memoirs of Ireland* (Belfast 1990-98), forty volumes.

9 See the recent edition of Kenneth Nicholls' *Gaelic and Gaelicised Ireland in the middle ages* (Dublin 2003), pp138-9.

10 See Griffith's *Valuation* published by Eneclann in Dublin: http://www.irishorigins.com/ . Other townland databases can currently be accessed such as at http://www.seanruad.com/

11 Donegal County Development Board, *County Atlas 2001*, Maps 16-18.

12 See S T Carleton, *Heads and hearths: the hearth money rolls and poll tax returns for County Antrim 1660-69* (Belfast 1991).

13 See Jean Graham, 'Rural society in Connacht, 1600-1640' in N Stephens and R E Glasscock (eds), *Irish geographical studies in honour of E. Estyn Evans* (Belfast 1970), pp192-208.

14 R A Dodgshon, *From chiefs to landlords: social and economic change in the Western Highlands and Islands*, c1493-1820 (Edinburgh 1998), p141.

15 This was envisaged for Scotland by Dodgshon, *ibid*. pp40-42.

16 T E McNeill, *Anglo-Norman Ulster* (Edinburgh 1980), p89.

17 The renditions of the names, however, are extremely difficult to reconstruct according to Bishop Duffy, Monaghan.

18 Liam Ó Buachalla, 'Placenames of north-east Cork' in *Journal of the Cork historical and archaeological society*, LIV (1949), pp31-34 and 88-91.

19 P Duffy, 'Social and spatial order in the MacMahon lordship of Airghialla in the late sixteenth century' in P Duffy et al (eds), *Gaelic Ireland: land, lordship and settlement, c1250-c1650* (Dublin 2001), pp 134-6.

20 See J H Andrews, 'The maps of the escheated counties of Ulster, 1609-10' in *Proceedings of the Royal Irish Academy*, lxxiv, sect.C (4), 1974, pp 133-170; 'Survey of Com. Monaghan' in *Inquisitionum in officio rotolorum cancellariae Hiberniae asservatarum, repertorium* (Dublin 1829), xxi-xxxi. P J Duffy, 'The territorial organisation of landownership and its transformation in county Monaghan, 1591-1640' in *Irish Geography*, 14, 1981, pp1-26.

21 R C Simington (ed), *The Civil Survey: counties Donegal, Londonderry and Tyrone*, Vol III (Dublin 1937), p403.

22 Duffy, 'Social and spatial order', *op. cit.*, pp128-9. In north Meath, lands belonging to the See of Armagh were divided into four and eight 'poles', though many of them emerged later as fewer townlands; see R C Simington (ed), *The Civil Survey: county Meath*, vol V, xxii, and p335.

23 Bath papers, Longleat, Irish box 1, William Smith's survey, 1612; Dodgshon, *Chiefs to landlords*, p125.

24 See P J Duffy, ' Patterns of landownership in Gaelic Monaghan in the late sixteenth century', in *Clogher Record*, X, 1981, pp306-310.

25 In Crawford and Foy (eds), *Townlands in Ulster*, p139

26 Sandra Millsopp, 'A townland study: Bangor, Co Down' in T Canavan (ed.), *Every stoney acre has a name*, p42.

27 Simington (ed.), *The Civil Survey: county Kildare*, Vol VIII, pp xxv-xxviii.

28 *Ibid*. p xxvii

29 Simington, *Civil Survey: Donegal, Londonderry and Tyrone*, p xviii.

30 Quoted by Simington, *Civil Survey: Kildare*, p xxvii.

31 McErlean, 'The Irish townland system', p322.

32 P J Duffy , 'Farney in 1634: an examination of Thomas Raven's survey of the Essex estate' in *Clogher Record*, XI, 1983, pp245-56.

33 Simington, *Civil Survey: Donegal, Londonderry and Tyrone*, pp398-9.

34 *Ibid*., p382.

35 *Ibid*., p310; 'Owen O Quiggerie' is most likely *Abhann coig chríoch*, marking an important historic boundary in the diocese of Clogher.

36 For a multimedia reflection of names and places in county Mayo, see the CD-rom *Dún Chaochán, landscapes, seascapes, placenames, stories, songs* (Belmullet 2000). For a comprehensive collection of traditional songs and stories from south-east Ulster, see Padraigín Ní Uallacháin, *A hidden Ulster: people, songs and traditions of Oriel* (Dublin 2003).

37 See John B Cunningham (ed.), *The letters of John O'Donovan from Fermanagh* (Belleek 1993), p56.

38 Séamus Ó Ceallaigh, *Gleanings from Ulster history* (Draperstown 1995, first edition 1951), pp56-7.

39 See the well-executed reproductions of valuation lists and their accompanying maps of townlands and farms in Crawford and Foy, *Townlands in Ulster*.

40 See W H Crawford, 'The significance of landed estates in Ulster, 1600-1820' in *Irish Economic and Social History*, XVII (1990), p61; J S Donnelly, 'The Kenmare estates during the nineteenth century' in *Journal of the Kerry Archaeological and Historical Society*, (21), 1988, pp5-41:16; P J Duffy, 'Management problems on a large estate in mid-nineteenth century Ireland: William Steuart Trench's report on the Shirley estate in 1843' in *Clogher Record*, XVI (1997), pp101-122.

41 R J Scally, *The end of hidden Ireland: rebellion, famine, emigration* (Oxford 1995), pp12-16.

42 My grandfather had a story about *his* grandfather working with horses in a field in Cornabroc in Monaghan (around the 1830s) when an Orange band from nearby Creighanroe marched through. He asked them not to bang the drum or they would frighten the horses. This had the opposite effect, so he let go the reins, jumped over the ditch and put his spade through the drum, which was a signal for a general riot. 'There never was an Orange march through Cornabroc again', he said.

43 P Ó Gallachair, 'Notes on Dromore parish, County Tyrone' in *Clogher Record*, IX, 1977, p268.

Save our townlands!

Cahal Dallat

My task is to mark the work of the Federation of Local Studies in its campaign to preserve our townland names. Historians, place-name experts, and many ordinary people, have highlighted the importance of our townland names as a significant part of our heritage which is accepted with pride by all sections of our community. From this it is argued that anything which would lead to the disappearance of the townland names should be resisted, and it is this determination not to accept a destructive alteration of rural addresses which has been the basis of the Federation's 'Townlands Campaign'. However it must be emphasised that we have positive rather than negative motivation. As the patron of the Ulster Local History Trust, Seamus Heaney, has written, 'The Townlands Campaign is manifestly something more than resistance to change for its own sake … but is rather about resisting a pressure to close something'.[1]

The Post Office authorities introduced a rural house-numbering and road-naming system in Northern Ireland in the years leading up to 1973. The system which, it was claimed, 'would ensure the speedy delivery of mail by changing rural addresses to road names and numbers', led to the belief that the new address, and only that, would be accepted. Under the new system every rural road was to be named and houses along each road were to be numbered in sequence. Gaps were left in the numbering sequence for houses not yet built! The official letter, sent out to occupiers, indicated that the new address should consist of a road name and house number only. As if to reinforce the notion that the townland name should not be part of the address, the *Post Office Guide* for 1976 included the following statement: 'The Post office requests that such superfluous information [e.g. the townland name] should be omitted.' The impression was given that letters carrying an address other than the official one could be delayed, misdirected, or might not be delivered. This could be a frightening thought for members of a rural community who depended on the speedy delivery of milk cheques, various subsidy payments, welfare benefits and such like. It soon became evident that people were becoming reluctant to include the townland name in their addresses and the result was that knowledge of the names was beginning to disappear. As a result, rural children were becoming unaware of the townlands in which they or their neighbours resided.

One official argued that the Post Office was safeguarding the townland names by using them for road names. The flaw in this argument was that only one townland name could be used at the expense of the other townlands through which the road passes. An example of this is Whitepark Road in north Antrim which runs from Ballycastle to Bushmills, a distance of twelve miles, and passes though twenty-nine townlands.

It is the local authorities which actually have the statutory power to name streets and roads, or not to do so. The Post Office policy had to be exercised by persuading local authorities to spend a lot of money in erecting rural road signs – something which is not generally done in England, Scotland, Wales, or the Irish Republic. It is often accepted that it was significant that the road-naming system was introduced at a time leading up to the reorganisation of local government in 1973. Rural and Urban Councils were being disbanded and new District Councils were being established. It might be an over-statement to suggest that local government was in chaos, but certainly members of councils were in a state of limbo. Perhaps the District Councils were influenced by the acceptance of the scheme by the Association of Rural District Councils at a meeting held on 1st March 1968. Clearly councillors were unaware of the detrimental effect the new road-naming scheme would have on the heritage of townland names, which has existed for a thousand years. In addition the naming and numbering of roads was seen as a directive from a higher authority which had to be obeyed.

As a result, the Post Office's road-naming system slipped into place with only a few isolated protests from individuals. It was to be well into 1975 before the dissenting voice of the Federation for Ulster Local Studies was raised. This was then a new organisation embracing almost all of the local historical societies and field clubs in the province of Ulster. The Federation had been formally constituted at the New University of Ulster at Coleraine, on Saturday 10th May 1975. It is somewhat surprising that none of the local history societies which came together to form the Federation had made any previous protest about what was happening. However there is little doubt that the societies were concerned about the road-naming system which ignored townland names, but separately felt incapable of challenging the might of the Post Office, which had always been seen as a powerful expression of 'government'.

In 1976 the Federation issued and widely distributed a leaflet written by its Secretary, Brian Turner, under the title *The Post Office and Rural Addresses in Northern Ireland*. This challenged the Post Office scheme and asserted that it was 'insensitive and lacking in regard for the particular circumstances of Ulster. Its general concept is clearly wrong and divorced from the evolution and practical usage of this country.' For ten years members of the Federation objected to the implementation of the scheme which had catastrophic implications for the continuity of historical documentation, and for Ulster people's sense of spatial awareness. Much sympathy and agreement was aroused, but little practical action by those who mattered in local government, despite many deputations received to address them directly.

To quote from a retrospective article published in the Federation's *Ulster Local Studies* journal for Summer 1986:

> One of the first exercises to engage the Federation was the campaign to preserve our townland names. For the past ten years our members have been visiting District Councils, appearing on television and speaking on radio in an attempt to make people aware of the importance of retaining townland names in rural

addresses. The campaign continues and the Federation sent letters to all the candidates in the Local Government Elections in May 1985 asking where they stood on the question of reinstatement of townland names in rural addresses. The response was encouraging and we now look forward to action from those more than one hundred councillors who pledged their support at that time.[2]

With some honourable exceptions, we are still waiting. In spite of the pledges of support mentioned in the 1986 Journal only a few councillors took positive action to support the townland names. In one Council the minutes which recorded the authorisation of the road names were reported to have been 'burnt in a fire'. In another a councillor said that the Post Office file was so thick and complicated that the councillors thought they should pass it without discussion. More positively, Lisburn Rural Council had refused to adopt the names before reorganisation in 1973, but its decision disappeared without trace following its absorption in a bigger unit after 1973. In 1987 Down District Council adopted a resolution which expressed the opinion that 'the abandonment of townland names is detrimental to the preservation of our local history, inhibits administration in many spheres, and is confusing in its application ... ', but the desired return to the use of townland names was frustrated by the contradictory retention of the road names.

Fermanagh stood proudly out. Fermanagh has a large number of small townlands and Fermanagh people are perhaps more conscious of their value, and less influenced by suburban people who have moved into the countryside than is the case in other places. Fermanagh District Council refused to accept the Post Office's road-naming system. Mr Gerry Burns, Chief Executive of the Council, told the story at a seminar entitled 'Townlands - A positive picture' organised by the Federation for Ulster Local Studies at Greenmount Agricultural College, Antrim on Saturday 4th September 1989.

Mr Burns said that after all of his years of experience in Fermanagh he now had townland names burned across his forehead! He had empathy with his employers when they had resisted the Post Office. The councillors in Fermanagh did not agree on a great deal for some years, but they did agree to fight for their townland names, despite severe pressure from various sources. Several members of the Federation committee - Jack Johnston, Brian Turner and Cahal Dallat - attended a meeting of Fermanagh District Council and gave their advice and support.[3]

Despite the fact that the road names could not legally exist without being authorised by the Council several government bodies began to use them. In 1988 the Post Office indicated that it was proceeding with a postal code based on the road names and numbers. Mr Burns advised the Council to consider seeking a High Court injunction and the Post Office then decided that it would allocate codes to townlands and not to proceed with road names. This brought great rejoicing in Fermanagh and should also have enabled the commercially conscious Post Office to supply coding lists to junk mail firms.

In the following years the road-naming system continued to be paid for by local authorities in most of Northern Ireland, with some ineffective attempts to accommodate townlands. But in October 2001 Mr Kieran McCarthy, a representative from the Ards peninsula in County Down, moved a motion in the Northern Ireland Assembly to assert 'That this assembly calls on each Government Department to adopt a policy of using and promoting townland names in all Government correspondence and official documents.'[4]

Mr McCarthy rehearsed the case for townland names and received informed and eloquent support from all parts of the Assembly, speaking mainly in English, but also in Ulster Scots and Irish. It is now the policy of government in Northern Ireland to use and promote townland names.

What does this mean for those concerned for the value of the townland names and the sense of local spatial awareness which they give us? It is certainly a major advance for government to use the names. It remains to be seen if the wishes of government are complied with by the postal authorities and all the other agencies, insurance companies, credit companies, banks, and other commercial bodies who demand our addresses in order to supply services. Despite the widespread popular goodwill towards the preservation and continued use of our heritage of townlands, the continued existence of expensive road names and numbers remains the essential threat. In our increasingly suburbanised society many distant agencies will feel more secure with a number rather than a, to them, unfamiliar name.[5]

It is in this respect that the very modern technology which was first invoked as inimical to townlands could now accommodate everybody's needs. Those who have been puzzled as to how to preserve our townland identities in the modern world now have the tools to do it. It is possible to computerise anything we like. We should be able to construct post-codes in such a way as to supply the legitimate needs of the Post Office and its customers without inserting those road names into our addresses which inflict such destructive, if unintended, damage to our cultural heritage and our practical knowledge of the landscape.

Respect for our heritage includes the use of our townland names as the primary element in rural addresses. Persistence is required. Save our townland names!

Notes and references

1 Seamus Heaney, 'Preface' to Tony Canavan (ed), *Every Stoney Acre has a Name: a celebration of the townland in Ulster* (Belfast 1991) p. xii.
2 Cahal Dallat, 'The Federation for Ulster local Studies ten years on', in *Ulster Local Studies*, vol. 9, no. 22, Summer 1986, p222.
3 'Townlands – a positive picture' in *Ulster Local Studies*, vol. 12, no. 1, Summer 1990, pp39-40.
4 Northern Ireland Assembly debate, 'Townland Names', Monday 1 October 2001.
5 The Telephone Directory will print a rural townland address if you wish, and this can be requested by those who support the townlands.

The scholar on the stagecoach: John O'Donovan and the Ordnance Survey

Myrtle Hill

In our attempts to reconstruct the past, historians are heavily reliant on the work of others – observers, commentators, chroniclers and archivists. And of course the quality of the sources we inherit from them varies enormously in terms of detail, accuracy, contextualisation and understanding. This is particularly important as the twists and turns of history are recorded not only as matters of verifiable factual or material evidence, but in the more fallible vaults of human memory where they often take on a life of their own. Moreover, language – the medium we use to communicate - is itself not fixed, but a shifting, changing dimension of the historical process. So, what a pleasure it is to, albeit briefly, introduce a scholar and an enthusiast who, aware of the dilemmas, inconsistencies and fallibility of the historical process, not only made a unique and lasting contribution to the study of local history, but also serves as an example and an inspiration to amateurs and professionals alike.[1]

Born on his father's County Kilkenny farm in 1809, the seventh of nine children, John O'Donovan spent much of his childhood with the family of his well-travelled uncle Patrick, who passed down to him his love of Irish and Anglo-Irish history and traditions, and an enthusiasm for local history, topography and genealogy.[2] An intelligent and diligent student, his education, locally and later at a private school in Waterford, by building on his knowledge of the Irish language and introducing him to Latin, equipped him well for his future work with ancient manuscripts. By the time of his death at the age of 52, O'Donovan's achievements in research, translation and publication would secure his own place in Irish history – despite the lack of financial reward, which left his widow and orphans almost penniless. His academic prestige and influence were furthered by his appointment to the first Chair of Celtic Languages at Queen's College Belfast in 1949 and a year later recognition of his status was reflected in an honorary degree bestowed by Trinity College Dublin. Simply to list his publications would take much more space than that allotted to me here, though I should draw attention to what is generally agreed to be his masterpiece, *The Annals of the Four Masters*, which he edited and translated in seven volumes.[3] But this short paper will focus on only one aspect of O'Donovan's work – the twelve years between 1830 and 1842 which he spent with the Ordnance Survey project. This is the work for which local historians searching for clues to how life was lived before the catastrophic events of the 1840s are indebted to him.

In 1824 a House of Commons committee recommended a townland survey of Ireland, with maps at the scale of six inches to one mile; its purpose was to facilitate a uniform valuation for local taxation. The survey was directed by Colonel Thomas Colby with the assistance of officers of the Royal Engineers, three companies of sappers and miners, and a team of civil servants whose task was to help with sketching, drawing and engraving maps, and eventually, in the 1830s, the production of the Memoirs - written descriptions intended to accompany the maps, and to detail additional information. It is the breadth of this additional material, as the surveyors recorded their findings on the landscape, on buildings and antiquities, land-holdings, population and employment, which makes the Ordnance Survey Memoirs so valuable a source. Unfortunately, budgetary and other considerations brought the project to an untimely close before the work was completed, and with the memoirs for only one county – Londonderry – reaching the stage of publication. The task of making this wealth of detailed local information available to a wider readership was not comprehensively tackled until the final decade of the twentieth century. [4]

The impressive team of scholars engaged on this project included George Petrie, Eugene O'Curry and Clarence Mangan, but amongst these and other experts, the name of John O'Donovan is pre-eminent. His biographer, Patricia Boyne, claims that 'in topographical lore, sanity of judgment, breadth of scholarship, sympathy towards new ideas and discoveries, he surpassed all his Irish-speaking contemporaries'.[5] His specific brief was to examine the old Irish records and manuscripts to determine the correct place names to use on the new maps and enter his revisions and conclusions in the Name Books provided by the officers undertaking the survey. O'Donovan was indeed uniquely qualified for such a task, not only as 'a native of the country [who] spoke the language of its ancient inhabitants', but one who possessed, through his study of manuscript sources, an unrivalled knowledge of its past.[6]

But it was O'Donovan's work in the field which most revealed his own character and expertise. Starting in County Down in 1834 he and a few colleagues travelled through twenty-nine of Ireland's thirty-two counties, seeking out and quarrying the memories of the most informed local people, often the native Irish speakers, or 'aborigines' as he called them. O'Donovan knew that the correct pronunciation and local knowledge, and therefore the clue to the meaning of names which had often been corrupted, lay with those who used them every day. In his investigation of the spelling of some 144,000 names, including those for our 62,000 townlands, featured on the new Ordnance Survey maps, he took nothing on trust. Intent on accuracy, he cross-checked every source, drawing on his extensive knowledge of local and genealogical tradition to seek clarification of published and unpublished texts. The Field Name Books and the many letters which O'Donovan wrote back to the project's base at Mountjoy Barracks in Dublin's Phoenix Park contained profuse notes on his findings, but were not originally intended for publication. They are, however, a remarkable resource for today's local historians. In addition to the information required by the survey, he vividly described his own experiences as he travelled through the highways and byways of early nineteenth-century Ireland, before it was struck by the catastrophe of the Great Famine. Both his reflections on the past and these detailed observations on his own time - of which this brief paper gives only a flavour – make him a well-informed companion for all interested in Ireland's past.

The budget allotted to O'Donovan for his travels was meagre. It allowed for neither overtime nor sick leave, and his journeys were undertaken by foot, boat and coach – in the cheapest seats and exposed to the vagaries of Irish weather. It's difficult to select examples from the wealth of wonderfully vibrant descriptions he has left us with, but this is a typical snippet – the tale of a journey between Derry and Enniskillen in October 1834, on the outside of a horse-drawn coach, with a bunch of 'noisy and inebriated' fellow travellers. They were already benumbed by cold and wet - worse was to follow:

> … When we had arrived within two yards of Seean Bridge between Strabane and NewtownStuart, the lofty vehicle was sublimely upset and splendidly thrown into the ditch! …The accident was so sudden, and the fall so steep that I knew not for some minutes what had occurred; whether we were carried into the firmament by some unknown power or whether old Nick had come to carry us all, cold, drunk and sober, as we were to warm us! At last I observed that it was an accident brought about by the negligence of the driver, who let the right wheel slip into the dyke, within two yards of a dangerous and steep bridge! My feet were so numb with the cold that I knew not whether I was killed or not. However, I asked myself the following questions: - Am I killed? Am I crippled? Are my brains dashed out? I got up and found to my great satisfaction that no vital part was touched, and no injury done except a slight bruise of my left side and arm, which remain very sore yet. No material injury happened; but if the vehicle had advanced about three yards further, we would have been all dashed to death against, and over the bridge! I thank Providence for our escape.[7]

Things did not always improve on arrival at any particular destination. In County Clare, for example, he described his experience as consisting of 'wet turf, sleeping in bogs, damp beds, potatoes like turnips, half-baked bread, adulterated tea, 'no meat', broken pains [i.e. of glass] and paying 2/6 per diem for an office to write in'.[8] It's not surprising that he frequently suffered from ill-health, but his enthusiasm was not easily dampened.

While carrying letters of introduction to notable local figures, he was frequently dismissive of both their knowledge and lifestyle, and his usual practice was to seek out the schoolteachers, clergy, and Irish speakers whose views he felt would be of more value. He was particularly aware of the importance of that knowledge which comes with age, especially in the difficult area of dialect. One example will illustrate the difference made by pronunciation:

> In the parish of Tyrella there is a townland called Ballykinler, which Vallencey, Beauford, and in all probability O'Reilly, would have explained, 'the town at the head of the sea' (Baile Cinn Lir) but as soon as I heard it pronounced by an old Irishman I said it must mean 'the town of the candlestick', (horrid name!!) and silly conjecture for any sensible person! Be it so, say I – but turn to the fact. Look at Harris's *History of the County of Down*, and you will find … the parish of

Ballykinler the tithes of which were appropriated to Christ Church Dublin for WAX LIGHTS.[9]

A perfectionist himself, O'Donovan had little patience with predecessors whose work did not meet his own high standards. Again a single example will suffice. Writing from Trim, he asserted:

> Our Irish writers of the last century have been a set of ignorant and dishonest scribblers without one manly or rigorous idea in their heads. Vallancey, Beauford, Ledwich, Roger O'Conor, etc. were all either fools or rogues who were by no means fit to demonstrate the truth of ancient or modern history.[10]

Harsh words, but then the perpetuation of error is a serious matter.

I should think that even these brief examples demonstrate that O'Donovan was not only scholarly and efficient, but a robust and entertaining writer. His letters, which cover all but three of Ireland's counties, were deposited in the Royal Irish Academy, which regarded them as 'the most valuable accession ever made to their library'.[11] Highly readable and accessible, they powerfully depict the land and people of Ireland just before the Great Famine swept over them and, whether in their manuscript form or in later edited editions, they have proved a veritable goldmine of information for the local historian.[12] Moreover, his work on tradition, history and mythology impacted not only on local and national history but, by influencing the work and stimulating the imagination of such great creative writers as Stephens, Hyde, Lady Gregory and Yeats, provided 'the link between the Old Gaelic Culture and the full flowering of Anglo-Irish literature achieved in the Irish Literary Revival'.[13]

So as we engage in our own research, whether of archives or people, whether or not supported by grants, institutions or amenable publishers, we should perhaps spare a thought for the trials and tribulations, enthusiasms, expertise and achievements of those who have gone before, particularly John O'Donovan, the scholar on the stagecoach.

Notes and references

1 Patricia Boyne, *John O'Donovan: a biography* (Kilkenny 1987); John B Cunningham (ed.) *The Letters of John O'Donovan from Fermanagh* (1993): (also on CD Rom).
2 Boyne, op. cit., p3.
3 John O'Donovan (ed. & trans.) *Annala Rioghachta Eireann: Annals of the kingdom of Ireland by the Four Masters, from the earliest period to the year 1616. Edited from MSS in the Library of the Royal Irish Academy and of Trinity College Dublin with a translation and copious notes*, 7 vols. (Dublin 1848-51; repr. Dublin, 1856; repr. Dublin, 1990).
4 The *Ordnance Survey Memoirs of Ireland* have been published in forty volumes by the Institute of Irish Studies, Queen's University, Belfast, in association with the Royal Irish Academy, Dublin, between 1990 and 1998. Patrick McWilliams' full *Index to Ordnance Survey Memoirs of Ireland Series –People and Places* was published in 2002.
5 Boyne, op. cit., p xiv.

6 As Petrie informed him 'You are qualified in a way that no other investigator is.' Boyne, op. cit., p40.
7 *Ibid.*, pp36-7.
8 *Ibid.*, pp32-3.
9 *Ibid,,* p26.
10 *Ibid.*, p43.
11 Michael Herity (ed.), *Ordnance Survey Letters Donegal* (Dublin, 2000), pp. xxi.
12 Michael Herity discusses the subsequent history of the Letters, *Ibid.*, pp. xx-xxii, and has himself edited the most recent volumes. In addition to the Donegal volume, *Ordnance Survey Letters Meath, Ordnance Survey Letters Down*, and *Ordnance Survey Letters Dublin* were published in Dublin in 2001.
13 Boyne, op. cit., pp129-32.

James Maguire of Ederny, County Fermanagh, sang songs about people and places.

What the Ordnance Survey can do for you

Stan Brown

Background

Both the Ordnance Survey of Northern Ireland (OSNI) and the Ordnance Survey of Ireland (OSi) are today very different organisations from when the Ordnance Survey first began in this country in the nineteenth century. That change has involved a major shift from field surveyors with their theodolites, and cartographers with their painstakingly produced paper maps, towards digital technology which they could not have imagined.

Early in the nineteenth century it became obvious that the local taxes in Ireland, which were called the County Cess, and based on townland units, were inequitable. Successive committees of the House of Commons debated the problem, and found that, although the names and outlines of townlands were assumed to be well known, the acreages and rateable valuations were doubtful. On the recommendation of the Spring Rice Committee, and born out of the need for accurate land measurement for valuation purposes, the Ordnance Survey in Ireland was established.

Thomas Colby, after whom the current OSNI building in Stranmillis, Belfast, is named, was chosen to undertake this task. He spent many years in Ireland establishing the Survey, and also found time to marry a Derry girl. The initial survey work, when completed in 1846, was the first detailed large scale mapping of any country in the world.

The Ordnance Survey is in essence the custodian of boundaries. Its official role in Boundary Surveys was set out in the Boundary Survey Act of 1854. Although the official Boundary Surveyor is the Commissioner of the Valuation Office, this is an historical accident - OSNI do the work.

At the time of the partition of Ireland, the Ordnance Survey was split into three separate parts, one each for Great Britain (OSGB), Northern Ireland (OSNI) and the Republic of Ireland (OSi).

OSNI's role today is as a government agency within the Department of Culture, Arts and Leisure (DCAL). It is a supplier of mapping (paper and digital) to national, regional and local government, private industry, value-added resellers, academics, researchers, publishers and the general public. OSNI data underpins much of the Northern Ireland economy and acts as a base reference for all Northern Ireland spatial data.

Technique and product

Historically, surveying was based on triangulation and the measurement of base lines by chains, rods, or tapes, and then the measurement of angles by theodolite. A network of smaller and smaller triangles was built up from the initial base line. It was of course a very time consuming exercise, as was the other end of the process, the making of maps. Cartography involved fine draftsmanship and required extreme patience and attention to detail. It took months for a single sheet to be produced: a thing of beauty and a joy forever.

However OSNI's mapping today is firmly in the digital era and is centred on the concept of Geographical Information and data. The traditional paper map is just an analogue method of displaying the data, but the concept is the same.

Over 80% of information has a spatial element and is concerned with questions such as:

Where is ...?

Where am I ...?

How do I get to ...?

Where is the nearest ...?

How do different areas compare ...?

What is located here ...?

What was located here ...?

How many people live within x miles of here ...?

How far away is ...?

What total area is occupied by ...?

What has changed in this area ...?

Who owns ...?

How does this variable relate to that one ...?

What shape is the land here ...?

OSNI's surveying nowadays is carried out by over 40 field surveyors using electronic theodolites, laser range finders, satellite positioning and pen computers to capture and manipulate the data. This data is very effectively supplemented by high resolution aerial stereophotography, with the images that are produced being used within OSNI's Photogrammetry section to update directly the digital database and to add land elevation or height information. The cartographic process is, at large scales of 1:1250 and 1:2500, an automatic process with the maps being directly derived from the digital database, some of which are updated daily. At smaller scales (1:50,000 and 1:250,000) the technique of

OSNI field surveyor at work.

computerised generalisation is used to make the map.

The digital database holds data in what is known as 'vector' format, where details about every point line and polygon (collectively known as 'features') on the map are linked directly (attributed) to the feature itself. The features represent something in the real world (past or present). Whatever the mapping scale, the data is held in separate layers on the database and can be manipulated using special software known as Geographical Information Systems (GIS), which allows maps to be viewed at different scales and automatically aligned. Some maps are generated as complete images and are digital equivalents of OSNI's well-known paper maps, such as the 1:50,000 Discoverer Series. These images are called 'raster data' and although they don't carry digital information about all the features on them, they are 'aware' of the location of their every pixel. GIS software also allows specially processed aerial photography to be merged with, or underlaid beneath, mapping so that they match exactly. The OSNI large scale database and the point addresses for any building can be superimposed on the base map and/or the photography. The power of GIS lies in its ability to link the mapping on screen to virtually any other external database. Tables and lists from almost any source, once converted into a format such as an Microsoft Access database or an Excel spreadsheet, can easily be linked to the map through what are know as common identifiers, including the location (which is a numerical code giving accurate positional coordinates). The digital map and its linked data within a GIS are therefore 'intelligent' and can thus be 'interrogated'. Data from both Northern Ireland and the Republic of Ireland is displayed on the same map projection system, (a type of Transverse Mercator projection) termed 'the Irish grid', which essentially describes the location of any point in Ireland as being a certain number of metres east and north of a zero-zero reference point off the south-west of Kerry.

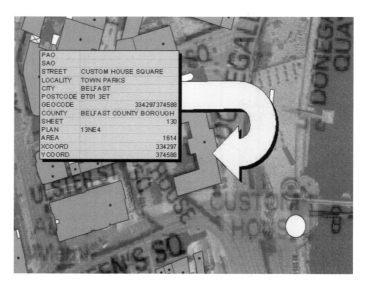

The OSNI large scale database and the point addresses for any building can be superimposed on the base map and the photography. GIS allows the map's features, such as the address, to be linked to any other external database.

GIS is a thus a powerful tool for researching, analysing and outputting information from diverse sources. It enables activities that, without it, would be very labour-intensive, or even impossible. Historical GIS, which brings together historical data, digitalised historic mapping and modern mapping, enables users to compare information over time and is now used in many countries.

There is no real limit to the number of databases that can be linked geographically in this way, using a GIS, and including, of course, historical data.

The aerial photography mentioned earlier is taken in stereo; because of the forward movement of the plane between the individual shots, they overlap each other by about 60%. From these stereo images, using special software, a 3D computer model can be created, like a fine wire mesh model of the landscape. The photography itself can then be automatically draped over this virtual model and physical features whether current, historical or planned, can added and visualised.

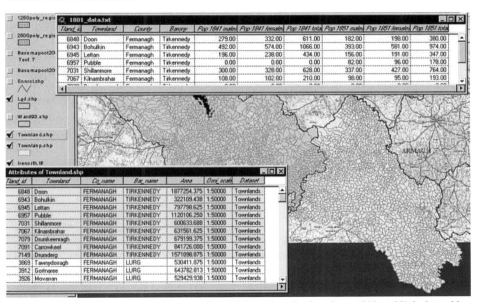

Townland datasets from counties Fermanagh and Monaghan displayed on a GIS and linked to tables.

The GIS (Geographic Information System) mentioned earlier is made up of a) hardware, b) software and, c) data. Individuals and organisations regularly use GIS for all sorts of applications.

Tables of information can be related to graphics (maps) allowing a graphic representation. For example, by linking and merging tables, so called thematic maps can be instantly produced to show densities, trends, and locations. An example might be a map showing population density changes in townlands before and after the Famine.

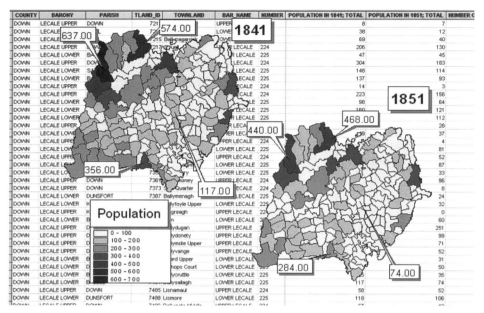

Thematic mapping derived using GIS and tabular data on population changes in the Lecale peninsula, County Down, before and after the Great Famine.

If all the different data is registered to the common framework of the Irish Grid, information from different sources can be shared. Older maps can be scanned and adjusted to the modern projections (a process known as 'rubber sheeting') and can be compared directly in overlay form with the current mapping. Townland boundaries, which are an OSNI digital dataset in their own right, can be displayed and used to interrogate the same data.

Access and use

It is important to understand the rules governing access and use of mapping data from the Ordnance Survey of Northern Ireland. OSNI have what is known as Delegated Authority from Her Majesty's Stationery Office, which essentially requires OSNI to control and protect Crown Copyright while allowing access to copyright mapping materials and data. OSNI are obliged to treat all users according to transparent and consistent rules. Old paper maps (over 50 years old) are out of copyright and incur no cost to use or copy, although a scanned and 'rectified' digital copy of it, which has been adjusted to match current mapping, is a newly created product and therefore does have its own copyright. In the case of paper maps that are within their copyright period of 50 years, up to four A4 copies can be used for private study or research, with no infringement of copyright being committed. There is no need for royalties but a © acknowledgement should be displayed. If there is no initial intention to publish but later you change your mind, then you should use the proper procedure for publishing.

If you intend at the outset to publish, then the use is not 'private' and a copyright licence will be needed initially, followed later by a publishing permit before going to print. If the project is going straight to publication, only a publishing permit is required. Obtaining these permits from OSNI is not difficult, or indeed prohibitively expensive. For any queries consult the OSNI website on www.osni.gov.uk or contact us by phone.

OSNI can supply copies of historical maps, modern paper maps, 'address centred extracts' and plots, all in paper format, as well as digital data files on CD or DVD of raster and vector mapping at all scales. The complete townland vector dataset is also available. In 2004 OSNI is commencing its web access project, which will allow digital mapping of many types to be remotely accessed on the Internet or special extranets. By 2005 almost all products (paper and digital) may be ordered on-line and digital products directly downloaded.

What about GIS costs? The software is available from several software providers at prices ranging from about £1000 - £5000 per licence for full function products. Some freeware is available with basic GIS functionality and can be downloaded from the Internet. The software (both full and cut-down versions) runs well on a modern PC or laptop.

For those computer owners who already have Microsoft Office, Excel spreadsheets can also be used quite easily to produce thematic maps, although full GIS functionality is not possible by this route. There are also GIS consultants within Ireland, North and South, who can advise on GIS use and who do specific work for clients. OSNI is itself currently considering trialling and developing some GIS charged services. A full price list of OSNI's mapping data (digital and paper) can be found on our website.

If you want to look at GIS being used by historians, examples can be seen by searching under 'Historical GIS' on an Internet search engine. The entry costs to digital mapping are not prohibitive. A fairly good modern PC will suffice and the output can be easily incorporated into reports or papers.

This short contribution is intended to demonstrate that both OSNI in Belfast and OSi in Dublin have data resources and expertise of value to historians. Whether you are using traditional paper or digital maps in your work, both Ordnance Surveys in Ireland are keen to help.

Townland: The hedged bet

Tess Maginess

What I had in mind with this title was to doff my cap, tacky of myself, at the word 'boundaries' in your august, faintly threnodic, conference title. (It says Yeats to my ear.) A hedge, as you all know rightly, is a class of a boundary. Many of the hedges about our farm are gone now, thanks to that great Extensification Imperative in the 60s and 70s when the Ministry Men (as they are **still** called) dispensed, after a sheaf of paperwork, grants for ripping out bushes and hedges to make the whole thing handier for the tractors. What has remained, in the line of hedges? One maybe three or four hundred years old – brave going for a bit of a whitethorn.

So part of what I want to squint at is the great big sea of Time. And the other thing I want to take your mind about is how different writers expressed their attitude to townland in terms of the metaphorical sense of 'boundaries'.

Now, if we can have a while's crack first about Time. An old woman, a 'friend' of my own, who lived - long after the most of the people had raised the roof and put in iron windows and made the hayloft into a yellow distempered bedroom, or got grants after that again to put up the wee bungalow, - in a whitewashed thatched house (not a cottage – that was a thing the 'Ministry Men' put up), used to say; 'There's terrible changes.' Many's a time my Da used to repeat this mantra in full parodic dramatic pathos. But for Margaret Mary, the word 'terrible' meant more than what we would have it mean in our townland – 'big' (an intensifer, an adjective), but 'terrible' in the full bore Yeatsian 'mere anarchy is loosed upon the world' chiliasm.

Had somebody took my Da in hand they would in no time, up in the city, have fashioned him into a comic writer – in the Irish sense of the word.

Now, how do writers, meditating in some way or other, about townlands, handle the question of time? If we look at Carleton, for example, we see in the *Traits and Stories* a sense of timelessness, but he is throwing the stories back to his own childhood. In *The Black Prophet*, written in 1848, we hear an account – and an anatomy of famine. Again, the story is thrown back thirty years or so. While the tone in *Traits and Stories* may at times be nostalgic, in *The Black Prophet*, it is both acerbic and supplicatory – for Carleton is exhorting the readership (The Pale, and the coffee houses of London), not to repeat the mistakes of history. No go? So time is repetitive or circular in a nightmarish way. What happens in the townland has *not* changed because the great powers in Dublin Castle, and more locally, have not analysed and learnt from the tragedy of the past.

Kavanagh's sense of time is, in some respects, like Carleton's in *Traits and Stories*. The townland was and is. It does not change. That, for Kavanagh, is both its attraction and drawback. The persona of *The Great Hunger* or Shancoduff will do the same things that he did twenty years from the now of the poem.

Of course, there were 'terrible' (and not so terrible) changes in Inniskeen over the course of Kavanagh's time. But that would not have suited. It would not have suited because the *urban* cultural establishment would not have appreciated the notion of change. The whole beauty (not a terrible beauty, just pure unadulterated beauty – which is the *raison d'etre* of art) of the country, *la campagne*, is that it *is* timeless. No good leaving 'the pavements grey' just to find the same litter strewn pavements in the middle of the west of Ireland.

Kavanagh heads up to Dublin and, cute boy as he was, realised this, just as Carleton did before him (except for the little local difficulty of *The Black Prophet*).

To put this another way, the literary and, in a broader sense, cultural constant of the country was (and is) a *space* that is 'other' to the city and town. That means that it is required to be *opposite* to the city – whereas the city is all rush, rush and change, the country is *projected* as timeless, easy going, changeless. It is also supposed to be full of 'characters' like Crazy Jane, Paddy Maguire, Raymond na Hatta, Buckramback the Dancing Master. As to townland – well now that is a bit *too* specific, just keep it 'country' now like a good chap. Keep the boundaries sharp between city and country. Both Carleton and Kavanagh did, of course, manage to 'widen the discourse' somewhat and insert on the pastoral map, place names, some awkward sounding, some astoundingly mellifluous, some just plain weird. Heaney does a great – if not entirely successful – job of 'sounding out' these names to a now literate rural audience, as well as the historical urban audience, which was near enough all there was in Carleton's time and maybe even in Kavanagh's time. Books were a ferocious luxury.

But Carleton, Kavanagh and Heaney are part of two worlds – the townlands and the city and – as writers – cannot but be influenced by the literary and cultural connections in terms of the presentation of the country. So, in writing from 'inside the margins' as men reared in townlands, they cannot but be on a hard pad, and to trudge or slide down it means trying to reconcile urban, pastoral, literary, high art images of the rural world with their own experience of it.

Well, they may have not altogether got the time thing right (a failure to record change), but then poetry, writing, is supposed to be timeless and you need to avoid the trap of the ephemeral.

However, what they did do was to create a greater awareness of the boundaries between an urban, pastoral view of the country and the reality of it.

Take a poem like 'From Tarry Flynn':

On an apple ripe September morning
Through the mist-chill fields I went
With a pitch-fork on my shoulder
Less for use than for devilment.

The threshing mill was set-up, I knew,
In Cassidy's haggard last night
And we owes them a day at the threshing
Since last year. O it was delight.

To be paying bills of laughter
And chatty gossip in kind
With work thrown in to ballast
The fantasy soaring mind.

The both veins are there, in that poem.

On the one hand, the urban, high art, mystical stuff (or guff), and on the other, the particularity of Cassidy's haggard and, hovering between the two - the (insider) sense of work to be done and the (outsider) sense of surveying the scene as an outsider; 'Less for use than devilment'.

Of course, poor oul' Paddy does not quite get up to the much promised devilment, being a poet and all, unlike my Da, who achieved the devilment, but not the (published) writing.

In Kavanagh, as in Heaney, the job is to break down over the boundaries, slither or bore through a hole in the hedge carrying a book on your head and a pitchfork (or a spade) between your finger and thumb. Looking very particular about you, noting the lines in some man's face or recording the cadence of his speech or the sound of the name of that townland, but crossing also from the inside margin to the wider, urban world containing literature – and audience.

And this plays out in another way – the hedged bet, that sense in which, from an inside marginal perspective, the view of the townland is *both* celebratory and condemnatory.

There is its universality (its parochialism in the Kavanagh sense), extending, possibly beyond lyricism to transcendence. And there is the narrowness (its provincialism in the not Kavanagh sense), narrowness, possibly beyond petty conservatism to isolation, intolerance. The condemnation of the 'oddity' who dares to look that bit too close and that bit too quizzically at blackthorn blossom or great teas or Ministry Men or the attitude to gay people or horrible bungalows or the end of ceilidhing or the tramping of farmland by men in a big way of business or the young ones taking drugs and not visiting their oul' 'friends' or satellite TV or gents with smug voices ruling out the working of bogs or the talk of 'our sort' or the cutting down of a plum copse.

So, there are always boundaries in the townland's heart and in the heart's townland. And, I hope, there will always be a hedge or two for me to bet on the future of the townland as a palimpsest – a series of inscriptions; that know, comically, about time, that know about change, that know about my Da's comic perspective that mimicked and twisted and could tell a peewheet from a cuckoo, a thrush from a finch, a gain from a loss.

Kilavoggy: A lane in Leitrim

Bryan Gallagher

My uncle was 53 when he and his young family emigrated to New York from a hungry mountainside in North Leitrim.

He had left it too late.

They said that at the foot of the aeroplane steps he stopped and made an attempt to go back.

Along with the good navy blue suit, the shirt with detachable collars, the box of collar studs and the pair of light boots, he had packed his fiddle and his bow, lovingly wrapped in sheets of newspaper. But he never played it in America and it stayed in a bottom drawer in yellowing sheets of *The Leitrim Observer*.

His letters were all about home with never a mention of his new life, and always, always he wanted to know what was the price of black cattle in Collooney Fair.

On the one occasion he came back, he made his way to the house where my father and he were reared, and with a pliers he pulled from the kitchen wall the nail on which we used to hang his fiddle. He brought it back to his New York home, hammered it into the wall there and that night, he played 'The Boys of Ballisodare' and hung his fiddle on it again.

I went back to North Leitrim a few years ago to visit the old house. I had been there once before as a child with my father. Now I carried my own son on my shoulders.

Round a bend up a steep lane I suddenly came face to face with an old man coming down. He stopped and looked at me and said 'Eddie.'

'That was my father's name,' I said.

'Well if your father was made young again, that's him walking up the lane.'

He spoke in that courtly way you only find in country places, and he turned round to walk back a bit with me and show me the way. He kept looking at me as if he couldn't believe his eyes.

'Would there be any chance that you would come back and do up the house?' he said. 'I would love to see someone above me on the mountain. There was smoke from all those chimneys,' he said, pointing out the ruined houses on the mountain face. 'I rambled in every one of those houses, but they're all gone now.'

'Did you never think of going away yourself?' I asked.

'I never was further than Collooney fair,' he said. 'Never further than the fair of Collooney.'

'What about your family?' I said.

'I have a son in Philadelphia,' he said. 'I was out to see him last year. I have another son in Los Angeles. I went out to him the year before. It's on the far side of America. The lane's bad but it's dry underfoot. Mind the little fellow.'

Gentle regular undulations of the grass were all that marked where my uncle's garden of brown sharp-edged ridges had been. Nettles and brambles were growing up to the open doorway. The boy wrinkled his nose at the smell of the calves in the kitchen.

And through the broken window I could still see the nail hole in the wall and the tracks of his pliers in the flaking pink distemper.

When I had seen enough, I turned to go.

The old man was waiting for me at a gap in the hedge. He had a paper bag in his hands. 'There's some apples for the boy. My two lads always liked them. You were always a fine big man, Eddie.' And he was gone through the gap in the hedge.

I didn't know if he was sane or mad. It was a strange and unsettling conversation.

In the car when I opened the bag, the apples had hard cracked skin and black spots from years of neglect, but the flesh inside was sweet and wholesome.

And as I looked at them I realised that the old man had not spoken to me at all.

He had been talking to a ghost, the ghost of a long dead neighbour that he had met walking up a lane in Leitrim.

Locality in literature

Eugene McCabe

This is a huge subject. We could spend a lifetime alone studying Homer and local references. He was the first great lyrical and epic poet. As a historian, journalist and moralist he is of special interest to us because Joyce used his *Odysseus* as a structure to explore a day in the life of Dublin and some Dubliners, three thousand years later. We then sail on from the Father of European literature to Virgil, 70 BC, and the Roman Empire under Augustus. There are over 200 place names indexed at the back of his major work *The Aeneid*. Then to the most influential book of the last two millennia, the Old and New Testaments. Apart from the sacredness of text, it is also a supreme work of literature, saturated with verse and the poetry of place names familiar to all Christians since childhood. Nazareth, Bethlehem, Galilee, Calvary, and the innumerable landmarks of Israel and Palestine that we now hear about every other day on news bulletins. Jerusalem was first mentioned in the Book of Joshua. Its history covers a period of three thousand years. Its name, ironically, 'The City of Peace', can be found on an inscription five hundred years before the conquest of David.

Having arrived from Homer to the Bible in one paragraph it might be appropriate to pause and look. I did so by opening my Douay edition at random, roughly midway, at the Third Book of Kings, Chapters 9 & 10, to check for place names. The first few lines mention Israel, Jerusalem and Libanus, and down a passage or so we are told that Solomon (King David's son) is having 'a fleet built at Asiongaber and Aliath which is on the shore of the Red Sea in the land of Edom' and this fleet came to Ophir. That's quite a roll call of locations.

I read on. Solomon's canticle of canticles being one of the most beautiful love poems in literature I wanted to know more about the man. What I happened across in Chapter 10 was something I did not expect:

> And Solomon loved many strange women besides the daughter of Pharao, and women of Moab, and of Ammon, and of Edom, and of Sidon, and of the Hethites … And he had seven hundred wives and three hundred concubines and … His heart was turned away by women to follow strange gods: and his heart was not perfect with the Lord his God …

As the Fermanagh man would put it, 'For a wise man wasn't he very foolish!'

Checking further, I realised I had innocently committed the sin of bibliomancy; that is to say, the opening of the Bible at random and attaching consequence to the first passage that meets the eye. This practice led to such abuse that bibliomancy was proscribed under pain of excommunication by the Council of Vannes in 465, and reinforced a century later by the Council of Orléan, And what a literature and history has grown out of that town Orléan and its maiden, warrior saint.

Dante is my next great poet in line. We associate him with Florence, exile, and

Ravenna where he died and was buried. He chose Virgil as his guide and set his magisterial works in Purgatory, Heaven and Hell, not localities we are familiar with - yet! Even with a well annotated translation and a plethora of footnotes he's not an easy read – nowhere near as accessible as Boccaccio. The scope of his *Decameron* is no less than Italy in the fourteenth century. It is not great literature but it had a marked influence on both Chaucer and Shakespeare. They were attracted by the freshness of everyday language, the irreverence and the earthy style, as illustrated in, for example, *The Canterbury Tales* – no end of place names – and Shakespeare in *All's well that ends well*.

I had a look. Every first sentence of a Decameron story begins by naming a real village, town or city, except for one called 'One into Nine won't Go', which begins thus: 'Just near here there was (and still is) a convent with a very holy reputation which for it's own sake shall remain nameless.' Needless to say the tale is so full of the shenanigans of naughty nuns that the effect is more incredible than scandalous.

Then we arrive at Shakespeare. He's off the Richter scale in all literary departments. This is Shallow to his cousin Silence, one country J.P. to another; 'What price a herd of bullocks at Stamford fair?' What could be more colloquial, more real, more now?

I once overheard two farmers in Clones Co-op, one saying to the other; 'I see bacon got an awful slap in Cavan.'

'Aye, but strong bullocks is still strong money.'

Then and now, the price of bullocks, the price of bacon. The Stratford man could move easily from common, pastoral talk to images in the Duke of Burgundy's monologue from *Henry the Fifth*:

> Peace hath from her too long been chased,
> And all her husbandry doth lie in heaps,
> Corrupting in it's own fertility.
> Her vine, the merry cheerer of the heart,
> Unpruned dies; her hedges even-pleached,
> Like prisoners wildly overgrown with hair,
> Put forth disordered twigs; her fallow leas
> The darnel, hemlock and rank fumatory
> Doth root upon, while the coulter rusts
> That should deracinate such savagery;
> The even mead, that once brought sweetly forth
> The freckled cowslip, burnet and green clover,
> Wanting the scythe, all uncorrected, rank,
> Conceives by idleness, and nothing teems
> But hateful docks, rough thistles, kecksies, burs,
> Losing both beauty and utility.
> And as our vineyards, fallows, meads and hedges,
> Defective in their natures, grow to wildness,
> Even so our houses, and ourselves, and children,
> Have lost or do not learn from want of time,

The sciences that should become our country;
But grow, like savages, - as soldiers will
That nothing do but meditate on blood -
To swearing, and stern looks, diffused attire,
And everything that seems unnatural.

The quality of that Shakespeare is incomparable. The location, war and its aftermath, as unavoidable then as now and in the future, if there is to be one. With the burning Bush in charge the unlikely becomes every day more likely!

There are two modern writers for whom locality (in their major works) can be somewhere, anywhere, nowhere; an anonymous building honeycombed with rat run corridors and terrifying interrogation rooms as in Kafka, or a tree by a roadside, two men passing the time waiting and wondering about living, dying and God. It's too obvious to say who that is. But at that time there was Fascism, a world war, a holocaust and 70 million war dead. Beckett survived this on the run as a farm labourer, and as a resistance intelligence officer. Living with the very real risk of betrayal and death at any moment did not lessen his sense of humour, but the overall effect of Godot, humour aside, is that bleakest of bleak images: 'We are born astride the grave, the light gleams and we are gone.'

With themes as universal as that, locality is this planet and the behaviour of its dominant species, humanity, and what we think and feel about here, now and hereafter; the increasing sense that this world is less than a grain of sand in a universe so vast it defies comprehension.

Then we have the paradox of Arthur Miller who confesses somewhere that he reads almost nothing but dialogue in stories and novels. When he sees great wads of local description as in Henry James, Thomas Hardy, Proust, or even Tolstoy, he skips or closes the book and reaches for another. Reality for him consists of what people say to each other in a tense, unfolding situation - drama. Paradoxically his *Death of a Salesman* has, indirectly, a more vivid sense of New York than any film by Martin Scorsese. The character Willie Loman, or Low man, is dwarfed by the locality of the New York skyline, with buildings on such a vast scale that he 'Can't see the stars, not enough light to grow a carrot!' He has lost faith in himself, his family, and the culture within which he is struggling to survive. He is also losing his mind and is suicidal as the play opens. In that greatest of American twentieth century tragedies the locality of New York is no mere backdrop. It's a living presence as monumental as a mountain, as alive as a river, a landscape, or a flesh and blood character.

We could go on and on listing names where locality is all-important. With William Faulkner you can feel the tension, taste the fear which seems to grow out of the torrid weather and the racial sagas of his Mississippi. He says himself he was blocked as a writer until he discovered 'that my own little postage stamp of native soil was worth writing about.' That 'postage stamp of native soil' was Kavanagh's south Monaghan townland of Donaghmoyne near Inniskeen, now immortalised. And John Synge? Apart from the great plays his *Aran Journal* is a hypnotic description of an island people and their culture as fascinating today as the day it was published. Thomas Hardy? He was clearly as passionate and detailed about his Wessex as Synge was about his islanders.

And if they are passionate, Joyce is obsessive, and even more detailed. We all know what's been said; that if Dublin were obliterated it could be reconstructed by a close reading of *Ulysses*. That insistence on accurately naming names prevented the publication of *Dubliners* for ten years? The publishers at the time maintained that fiction was fiction. Why name real streets and house numbers, shops, statues, pubs, hotels, railway stations, and more worryingly, thinly disguised neighbours and family members. It's distracting for readers and could lead to libel actions! Joyce was patient and intransigent. To experience these stories nowadays it seems unbelievable that such changes were demanded. It was T S Eliot who remarked that, 'Our interest extends to Joyce's family, and as he intended, to his friends, and to every other detail of the topography and life of Dublin and the Dublin of his childhood.'   When *Dubliners* was completed he was twenty-three. It seems hard to believe that *The Dead*, 'One of the three greatest short stories ever written', (again that's Eliot's judgement) was created by someone scarcely out of boyhood.

Years back I came across a reference to townland in the correspondence of Jonathan Swift. He was ill humoured that day, castigating 'the Irish of all classes' for what he called 'their senseless use of the word townland to describe the most remote areas of this Kingdom when clearly the word means those lands adjacent to a town. Only in Ireland do they employ this foolishness.' As I read this cultural cuff on the ear I had to agree, reluctantly. You don't come across townland in English prose or poetry. And if you think about it, it does seem a bit odd. Now, many moons later, I decided to clarify the origin of the word with Samuel Johnson. He omits it entirely. I went to other dictionaries. Nothing. So I looked into the County Library in Clones where they have a *Concise Oxford English Dictionary*. And there it was, 'Townland: a territorial division commonly used in Ireland.'

Six words. Not very helpful. It began to look as if the Dean might be right. Finally I contacted a friend who has the six volume monumental edition of the Oxford English dictionary. The email came back by return with no end of quotes, illustrations and explanations. Here's a few: 'Townland'; from the Old English, 'tun-land', the land forming a 'tun' or manor; in England, manor lands; in Scotland, the enclosed land or infield of a farm; in Ireland, a division of land. These are slightly different interpretations of the same word, none of them implying 'that land adjacent to a town.' Its use was apparently dropped in Scotland and in Elizabethan English, but continued to have a particular meaning here in Ireland, and why not? This present volume of explorations and information gives it plenty of justification.

In the *Calender of State Papers, Ireland* in 1658 (that's before Swift was born) we have a reference to 'the survey of every particular townland'. In an Irish Act of Charles II in 1662 we read, '… the number of acres in each townland, village, bally or quarter. Two or three cabins joined together are sufficient to constitute a town and the land adjoining thereto is called a townland.'

Jumping ahead to modern times I quote from *Grania*, a work by Emily Lawless; 'Innismaan possesses but two townlands, containing six quarters each, with sixteen croggeries to every quarter and sixteen acres to every croggery.' How about Croggery! It's no use for scrabble. You won't find it an ordinary dictionary. I got back on to my friend. He was startled to discover it was not listed, but Emily Lawless knew what it meant, so if anyone here knows the OED will be delighted to hear from you.

I'm straying a bit. The point I'm making is that the great Dean was having a go; punching air, which he did on a daily basis, verbally or with his satiric pen. What I do think slightly strange is that he should fasten on a word which has such enormous resonance. His own townland of Laracor and its house near Trim was a small, beloved kingdom, a place to escape to from the forbidding deanery of Saint Patrick's in Dublin.

In Northern Ireland there is an effort to replace our place-names by numbers. My grandfather was born in a house in the townland called Corranny under Carn Rock in Fermanagh. On the rates bill it now says '129 Carnmore Road'. It's hard to imagine anything in a poor and beautiful landscape more lacking in imagination, more ludicrous. My grandfather had spent his entire working life in Glasgow, but every summer holiday he was back with family and neighbours in Corranny. In his notebook, which I still have, he kept a meticulous account of expenses involved with the upkeep of his house: thatching, hedge cutting, carpentry repairs, forge work on gates, with the names and townlands of the men who kept things tight and tidy for him. It's a dignified roll: James Mulligan of Corraghy, Tom Kelly of Knockmacarooney, Pat Grue of Greholia, Johnny Mohan of Follom.

The names are written in a copperplate hand. You can sense that he liked writing down these townland names. I first realised place-name significance when I was eight, nine, or thereabouts. I was sitting on the yard wall looking down on Corranny lake. My grandfather was leaning on the same wall beside me when, audibly and unmistakably, he broke wind. I think he was as startled as I was, but recovered his dignity by saying, 'This is one townland where you can do that!'

He could see I didn't understand. 'Corranny', he said, 'from the Irish, means hill of the wind.'

I see from a recent excellent history of Corranny school that Corranny in fact means 'Head of the marsh'. I bow to the accuracy of that explanation, but for me it will remain '*Corr na gaoithe*, Hill of the wind!'

Shirley, in his *History of the County of Monaghan* tells us there are 1853 townlands in the county, and all the thousands in Ireland have their histories, if we but knew them. In *Poems of the Dispossessed*, adapted from the Irish by Sean Ó Tuama and Tom Kinsella there are 106 place names indexed at the back, places and rivers, from the earliest times to the middle of the nineteenth century. Many of you will have read and will know them. The locality is all of Ireland and the literature from all of Ireland from the medieval 'Vain my visit to Lough Dearg', to the anonymous eighteenth-century lament, 'Kilcash'. Kilcash, by the way, was a great house near Clonmel belonging to the Butler family until well into the eighteenth century. Clearly, it came to grief. Brian Merriman's 'Midnight Court' is a blend of Boccaccio, Rabelais and Jonathan Swift. Locality in that epic satire, as in *Godot,* is an imaginary place where Irish men are docked and tongue-lashed by women for being useless lovers. Some of the women in King Solomon's royal dormitories would, I imagine, have identified with the spirit of that work. In fact there's so much of interest in that volume of poetic repossession that we're spoiled for choice. 'Lament for Art O'Leary' is a passionate love poem associated with Cork. No translation can either do justice to it or diminish its power, but the finest lyric by the blind poet Raftery gets an indifferent outing:

> I am Raftery the poet, full of courage and love,
> my eyes without light, in calmness serene,
> taking my way by the light of my heart,
> feeble and tired to the end of my road:
> look at me now, my face towards Balla,
> performing music to empty pockets.

The following is how Frank O'Connor interprets the same lines:

> I am Raftery the poet,
> Full of hope and love,
> With eyes without light
> And calm without torment
>
> Going west on my journey
> By the light of my heart,
> Weak and tired
> To my road's end.
>
> Look at me now,
> My face to the wall,
> Playing music
> To empty pockets.

That must be close to the spirit of the original. As an epitaph about blindness, poverty and approaching death it's inspirational. 'Going west' was an early Christian notion about how souls go to Heaven, our ultimate location - in an Irish context, to the Isles of the Blest. That volume, *Poems of the Dispossessed,* should be on everyone's shelf.

In and around all these concerns the value of an organisation like the Ulster Local History Trust, and indeed all balanced and well-edited historical societies, is immeasurable. The contributions to the Trust's previous conference in Monaghan in 2001 have been published in the book, *The Debateable Land*.[1] In that book, and in the context of Ulster borders of various kinds, Jack Johnston phrased an aim, '… to produce a new breed along the Border here - a breed of dispassionate historians.'

Brian Turner put it another way by saying, 'Four hundred years after the Plantation of Ulster we should be able to view the scene through a wider lens.' And Myrtle Hill, looking at the 'Second Reformation in Cavan' in 1820, rounds off a complex investigation by saying:

> If we have reached a clearer understanding of at least some of the multiple influences and pressures involved, then perhaps this, rather than a clear-cut definitive pronouncement on the rights and wrongs of the situation, is a valid and helpful, historical exercise.

Absolutely. These are wise and hopeful words which must in time bear fruit. Publications like *The Debateable Land* (not a dull piece in it) become part of a healing process by helping to light up the past with honesty. There is a great deal about the past that we all have to come to terms with; not just the great events, injustices, battles and brutalities on all sides, but many commonplace things we're ignorant about. The examples I'm going to give you are trivial and non-controversial, but here they are for what they're worth.

Some years back Jimmy Corr, a neighbour farmer cum contractor, arrived at my house with a question. He had American guests, far out kin. They were delighted with Tirnahinch. From the top of Jimmy's farm you can see Tirnahinch lake, the border river, Carn rock, and Flynn's round tower less than half a mile away. And of course the Americans were fascinated.

'Gee, ain't that somethin'!'

They wanted to see the tower up close, which they did, and then wanted to know its history. Was it a thousand years old? More? Less? Jimmy apologised and said all he knew was it was Flynn's tower, but added that he did know a man would know. To me he said, 'I'm all my life lookin' at that thing. It never crossed my mind to ask who built it or how old? You'd know its history I'd say?'

'Little more than you, Jimmy,' I told him. 'It belonged to Bensons before Flynns and away back someone told me it was a windmill built by one of King Billy's Dutch engineers.'

'King Billy!' he said. 'A Dutch engineer! That's powerful. They'll like that.'

'I was a child when I heard that Jimmy. Might be true, might not, but I'll find out for you.'

I phoned Philip Moore who thought the King Billy notion unlikely, but if I wanted details Pat Holland, another neighbour and teacher, was, coincidentally, researching the history of the tower. I got on to Pat. He arrived, and King Billy's engineer got the boot.

'It's nowhere near as old as that,' he said. 'It was built by Bensons in 1829 - a windmill, yes, used for finishing the spades forged by the Mac Mahons of

Shannock with their water mill near Lackey.'

As it happens Lackey bridge was on the edge our farm, Drumard, and the Spademill Mac Mahons were far out kin. 'Then', Pat went on, 'for whatever reason, the Mac Mahons and Bensons parted company. From that time on the windmill was used for grinding corn till the great wind of 1839. That wrecked nearly every mill in the country. After that it went dormant. It's been that way ever since.

That was clear, simple and, I'm sure, accurate. I thanked him and was wishing him well with his research paper when he said he had a question for me. 'You've written a fable for children about a squirrel, and every townland hereabouts gets a mention except Carraveetra, where *we* live?'

He was half joking, half in earnest. There and then I promised Pat that somewhere, somehow, someday I would incorporate Carraveetra into a piece of writing.

And now the promise has been kept. Carraveetra means 'the lower quarter', and gives me a faint echo of Paris and the Latin Quarter - except that no two locations under the sun could be more dissimilar!

Like Jimmy Corr I have a grave confession to make about my disregarding of local history. Long ago there was a Clogher Historical Society outing, a walk and lecture in the bottomlands adjoining Tirnahinch lake on our townland of Drumard. We were deep in silage elsewhere at the time. Clearly I'd missed the notification. I heard about it days later from a neighbour: 'There was fifty or more', he said. 'Men and weemen in their wellies with cameras and walkin' sticks.'

It seems Owen Roe O'Neill had an unhappy encounter in this lake area with the English forces, his first serious military setback. He retreated to Redhills. Sometimes when I look down on that boggy landscape I imagine the snorting of horses and battle cries, the beginning of the end for Hugh O'Neill's brilliant warrior nephew. But it's blood under the bridge now.

And there's still more on our little postage stamp of land. In a field called 'The Church Park' there's a circle of trees, and within that circle the remains of a small church and graveyard, the church of Saint Eachaidh of Clones. The late Patrick Mulligan (Co-founder of the Clogher Historical Society and previous bishop of this diocese) told me back in the fifties that he thought it was sixth or seventh-century. It comprises the remains a small central church and was probably surrounded by bee-hive cells where the monks worked, prayed, lived out their lives, died and were buried. I thought this fascinating and I'd like to see it researched in depth.

I'm tempted to talk in some detail about Patrick Kavanagh, but more inclined to resist. He's too obvious a choice. His work in both prose and poetry provides the best modern Irish examples of how location and literature combine. Again and again he conjures images that convey an unforgettable sense of place. That line from Shancoduff is haunting:

'When dawn whitens Glassdrummond chapel.'

Seldom can five words flood the imagination with such a sense of place, wonder, and beauty.

To finish now I'll go back two decades to when our second son, Patrick, was twenty years old in New York. It was a Sunday when he phoned and asked,

'What's it like at home now - the weather?'

'Raining', I said.

' It's raining here too in Manhattan.'

And we talked on. Near the end of the call he said, 'I've been looking down at the street here all morning, thinking about Drumard, going round and round every field in my head. I can see them all as clear as anything.'

After such an image of grieving it was hard to keep talking.

The sequel to that call is that Patrick is back here with his American wife and three children, living in Corranny in the house his great grandfather left over a hundred years ago on 'The hill of the wind'.

It's a happier ending than Columcille's. During research in 1969 I came across a poem called 'Columcille's Farewell' in Ennis library. I thought it exceptional. Carelessly I did not note the name of the book, the original Irish, nor the translator's name. I now know that it is in Manus O'Donnell's sixteenth-century 'Life of Colmcille' - *Béatha Colaim Chille,* but I don't know who made this particular wonderful translation. I've had it published elsewhere and ascribed to 'Author unknown'. The raven is the harbinger of death and Alba is Scotland. Ten locations are lovingly named. The voice is full of passionate heartbreak as he calls out to his beloved places and people - to Ireland itself. If there are two sadder lines in any language than the closing couplet I have yet to come across them.

Columcille's Farewell

How quickly my coracle speeds on,
The salt spray blinds my gaze,
I grieve on the trackless sea,
Sailing from Ireland to Alba of the ravens.

The cliffs grow small,
As through a mist of death my eyes look back,
I shall never see again,
The wives of Ireland or their men.

Gael, Gael oh precious name,
Broken is my heart within my breast,
Should sudden death overtake me,
It is for my great love of the Gael.

Beloved are Durrow and Derry,
Beloved is Raphoe in purity,
Beloved Drumhome of rich fruits,
Beloved are Swords and Kells.

Beloved to my heart is the West
Drumcliff and Culcinne strand.
Their salt mains on which the seagulls cry,
The bareness of their rocks and shores.

How cruelly my coracle speeds on,
Wrenching from my gaze the earth I love,
Oh God the bitter sea is teeming on my face,
Sailing from Ireland to Alba of the Ravens.

*Bronagh Higgins and
Conall Curran from
Monaghan.*

Ulster townlands on seventeenth-century maps

Annesley Malley

People who own land and property have usually wanted it to be mapped so that they could record their estates and boundaries. The Plantation of Ulster in the early seventeenth century, with its grants of confiscated land to incoming people from Britain who were then expected to organise estates, obviously made mapping essential. But it was also very difficult for strangers to do, and was only made possible in detail by using the knowledge of local people who told the surveyors the names and locations of the existing land divisions. Thus did the ancient townlands survive and come through the upheavals of the seventeenth century to form the basis of modern landholding at all levels.

Sixteenth and seventeenth-century surveyors in Ireland were first asked to survey large areas, some covering many counties, and that produced practical problems. The early maps were not very accurate as the surveyors could not measure large distances over difficult terrain with large forests, bogs, and hostile locals who attacked them. Some of these men lost their lives trying to survey parts of Ireland.

Late sixteenth century Irish maps by Robert Lythe, whose work was considered to be reasonably accurate, were copied by later surveyors like John Speed and Johan Blaeu. The practice of copying other surveyor's work led to the repetition of inaccuracies, and this is something to be conscious of when studying maps from this period. A simple example of this is on Johan Blaeu's map dated 1654, where he is still using the name 'County Coleraine', when it had been changed to County Londonderry in 1613.

Every landowner and tenant knew their land by its townland name. This naming of land was repeated within the townland where each field on the farm was given its own name for practical purposes. Survival and analysis of these field names is also important for the study of our landscape history. A very colourful example of an early Irish map showing such detail relates to the estate of Sir Walter Raleigh at Mogeely in County Cork in 1598, where all the fields are named, eg. 'The Parkes Close', 'The Oxe Lease', and 'The Warrenne'.

Maps were often made on a county basis. Early examples were County Monaghan, surveyed in 1590, and various maps were made of County Down in the 1580s.[1] When the six Plantation counties of Armagh, Cavan, Fermanagh, Donegal, Londonderry and Tyrone were distributed after 1600 some very good surveyors were brought over from England to make more detailed maps of smaller areas. One of these men was Richard Barthelet who made a map of the Province of Ulster in 1602 and then made a very detailed map of the area south of Lough Neagh and along the river Blackwater in 1603. This map is particularly good for showing major blocks of old woodland such as that in 'Clan-Brasil' in north Armagh and Killultagh in what became south Antrim.[2]

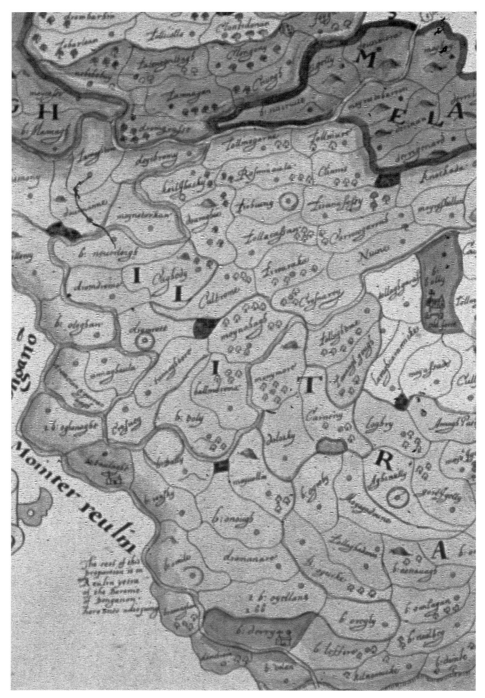

Detail from Sir Josias Bodley's 1609 map of the barony of Loughinsholin, recording its townlands. Moneymore (see next page) is near the centre.

In 1607 the large areas of the 'escheated estates' of the Earl of Tyrone and others had been sequestered by James I, and in 1609 the task of surveying all these lands was given to Sir Josias Bodley and a team of surveyors. Bodley had been in Ireland with Lord Deputy Mountjoy during the campaign against the northern lords and had surveyed many forts and towns for him. The task now was to survey the counties of Fermanagh, Tyrone, Cavan, part of Louth, Armagh and what is now south Derry. This survey was to be carried out by five surveyors who were under instructions as to what they should include on their maps. The maps were produced on a barony by barony basis and Bodley gave instructions to his surveyors to use local people in order to plot features and boundaries. He describes the method of surveying,

> For which we thought it our readiest course that…..we should call unto us out of every barony, such persons as by their experience in the country, could give us the name and quality of every ballibo, quarter, tate, or other common measure in any [of] the precincts of the same; with special notice how they butted, or mered interchangeably the one on the other.[3]

The maps that resulted from this detailed survey for four counties, and adjacent areas, were a colourful set of documents showing the old townland boundaries, names, churches, castles, monuments, bogs, rivers and woodlands. The names of the townlands are clearly given and many can be traced to modern townland maps today. An example is the area around the town of Moneymore in south Derry and the townland adjoining of Ballindrum, where the National Trust house of Springhill sits. This map of 1609 shows woodland in these townlands and that area was part of the old forest of Kiletra that covered south Derry. At Springhill today there are many trees, including a grove of fourteen old yew trees, ten of which measure over ten feet in circumference. This probably makes them much older than Springhill House, which dates from the 1690s.

The Ordnance Survey, in 1860, copied the original Bodley maps and many good reference libraries have bound volumes. The Public Record Office of Northern Ireland have a set and the Public Record Office in London have the colourful originals.[4]

One of the surveyors who worked with Bodley was Thomas Raven and he went on to undertake some very detailed estate surveys. He worked for Sir Thomas Phillips on the survey of the London Companies' estates in County Londonderry, completed in 1622, and then surveyed the estate of Sir James Hamilton in 1625 and 1626. This survey was very detailed and covered townlands from Holywood to Killyleagh in County Down. These maps were drawn by mapping small groups of townlands and many show woodlands and other features, including the lost village of 'West Holywood'. The present Holywood derives from the old village of 'East Holywood'. Thomas Raven went on to survey many other estates and so we have records of the townland names of the areas in which he worked. One particular map of his around Killyleagh Castle in County Down shows the old deer park, which goes back to the medieval period. Some of the blocks of woodland from this old parkland

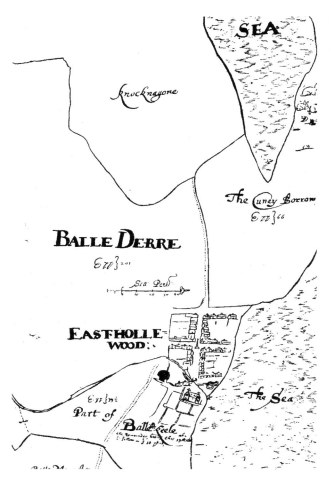

Copy of Thomas Raven's 1625 map of East Holywood, County Down. (From John Stevenson, Two centuries of life in Down, *Belfast 1920)*

still survive at Killyleagh.[5]

One of the few good things Oliver Cromwell did for Ireland was to leave behind the records of the Civil Survey completed in 1656, the Census of 1659,[6] and the maps of the 'Down Survey' by Sir William Petty. Sir William and his surveyors, who were mainly soldiers, had to survey all the counties of Ireland showing church property, forfeited land, and native freeholders lands, and they were to show each barony. Most of these maps include relatively few old names, but Petty's men were also to complete a map of each parish and they were to mark each block of land according to its type; ie. arable, pasture, woodland or bog. The area divisions were to be added in a table for each parish. It is in these tables that many townland names appeared, including some that have subsequently been lost. Many of Petty's Down Survey parish maps have now been lost, but the Public Record Office of Northern Ireland have copies for many parishes in the North, and also copies done by the land surveyor, Daniel O'Brien, in about 1780.[7]

Maps are fundamental to local historical studies. Examination of our early manuscript estate and parish maps will not only enhance appreciation of the antiquity and importance of our townland system, but also enable us to locate lost names. Careful attention to other features marked on the maps will also help us to see what our landscape was like over 300 years ago.

Detail from the Down Survey map of the parish of Glenarm, County Antrim, c.1660.

Notes and references

1 Colour photographs of these maps in the Public Record Office, London, were published in Michael Swift, *Historical maps of Ireland* (London 1999).
2 G A Hayes-McCoy, *Ulster and other Irish maps* (Dublin 1964); and 'Ulster 1602-3' in Swift, op cit.
3 J H Andrews, 'Maps of the Escheated Counties of Ulster 1609-1610' in *Proceedings of the Royal Irish Academy*, Vol. 74 (1974), Section C, p145.
4 Ordnance Survey, Ireland, *Maps of the Escheated Counties in Ireland 1609* (Dublin 1861).
5 D A Chart, *London and the London Companies 1609-1629* (Belfast 1928); and the original maps made by Thomas Raven of the townlands of Sir James Hamilton's estate in County Down are held by the North Down Heritage Centre, Bangor, County Down.
6 Robert C Simington, *The Civil Survey, AD 1654-1656, Vol 3, Counties of Donegal, Londonderry and Tyrone* (Dublin 1937); Seamus Pender, *A Census of Ireland, Circa 1659* (Dublin 1937. Republished with a new introduction by William J Smyth, Dublin 2003).
7 For information on O'Brien's work see J H Andrews, *Plantation Acres: an historical study of the Irish land surveyor and his maps* (Belfast 1985), pp85-86.

Caughoo and Cavan

Wendy Swan

My subjects are a townland called Caughoo[1] and a horse named after that townland; and also another part of Ireland, Lough Conn in County Mayo, a horse named after that lake, and the people involved. I will tell you how both these place names travelled beyond their boundaries to the famous racecourse at Aintree, Liverpool, and farther afield to Rome and the Vatican.

Caughoo is a townland in the parish of Kilmore, County Cavan. Caughoo (Irish, *cathadh*, 'winnowing') implies a place where grain was winnowed. Griffith's valuation in 1857 describes Caughoo as a 371 acre townland with 18 households. One of the households was that of the McDowell family which figures in this story. John McDowell is listed as having 40 acres 3 roods and 36 perches with a poor law valuation of £23-10-0.[2]

John McDowell had three sons. John Jr. remained at home and his descendants reside in Caughoo today. William and Richard emigrated to Australia where they found work in a diamond mine. When they had gathered some money together, they returned home and bought a jewelry shop on O'Connell Street, Dublin, called the 'Happy Ring House' and still owned by the family.

William the jeweller and his family were great horse lovers. His eldest son Jack bought a small two-year-old horse for 40 guineas at Ballsbridge sales in 1940. For a short while the horse grazed on the Caughoo farm and, remembering their origins, the McDowells named their horse Caughoo. Jack's brother, Herbert, a veterinary surgeon, trained the horse. After many successful competitions Caughoo was led into the enclosure at Aintree on a Saturday in March 1947 by Miss Mary McDowell, sister of the owner, and watched by their delighted mother.

1947 was the first year that the Grand National was run on a Saturday, at the request of the Prime Minister, Clement Attlee, in the interest of British Industry. Eddie Dempsey was the jockey who rode Caughoo that day. He came from Ratoath, County Meath, and it was his first time to take part in an English race. The groom was Ted Wright. The betting on Caughoo was 100/1.

The report of the race in the Cavan paper, *The Anglo-Celt*, stated that the conditions on the racecourse that day were terrible. The course was waterlogged with a heavy mist hanging over it. The thousands of spectators only got occasional glimpses of the horses as they galloped through the mud. Caughoo's colours of green, blue and white could be picked out as he took the lead three fences from home and went on to finish by 20 lengths in front of Lough Conn. At 100/1 you can imagine the return for money the family got. On their return home on the boat, the family took over the bar and treated everyone on board to drinks.

When the victorious racehorse arrived back in Dublin on the following Thursday, two bands played up O'Connell Street in front of him. On returning to the McDowell home in Sutton, the streets were decorated and bonfires blazed. A tremendous reception was given to Caughoo, the family, and to Eddie Dempsey, the jockey.

The following September Caughoo was brought back to Cavan to parade at Cavan Show, held in the townland of Kilnavar (Irish, *coill na bhfear*, 'wood of the men') overlooking the town. Admission to the show ground that day was two shillings.

When Caughoo died, the McDowell family had him buried opposite the hall door of their home in Sutton.

Due to the terrible weather conditions at Aintree on the day of the Grand National, we can understand how a rumour got around that Caughoo did not go round the four-and-a-half mile racecourse twice. It was said that because he was a small horse he stood in behind a hedge and when he found the horses coming round again he stepped out of the mist in front of the others and won the race.

Caughoo's success extended as far as the Vatican. On Friday 25th April 2003 an article was published on an Ennis web site entitled: 'A dream come true - Gift for the Pope'. It told the story of Mr Mungovan, an 83 year old retired farmer from Rathkerry, Inch, near Ennis, County Clare who had been in the habit of placing a small bet on the Grand National, the Lincoln and the Derby. His choice in 1947 was the horse called 'Lough Conn', but a fortnight before the race he had a dream. In the dream he thought he was in the presence of two men having a conversation. This conversation was about which horse would win the Grand National. One man said 'Prince Regent' would win. 'Nonsense,'said the other, 'Caughoo will run away with it.' On wakening the next morning, the name of the horse Caughoo stuck in his mind. He went out and bought the newspaper and there was Caughoo amongst the list of runners. Mr. Mungovan said that on the morning of the race he went to Ennis with £30-10-0. He put £30 on Caughoo with one bookmaker and 10/- with another. The first bookmaker laughed at him for betting so much money on Caughoo and tried to stop him making a fool of himself. But Mr Mungovan persisted with his bet and won £3,050. He sent £1000 of this money to His Holiness The Pope, through his lordship, Most Rev Dr Fogarty, for the starving children in Europe. Mr Mungovan heard nothing from the Vatican until September 1947 when he received a letter and a casket from Cardinal Nontine, the Papal Secretary of State. At the Pope's instructions he congratulated him on his good fortune and thanked him for the generous gift to the starving children. The casket contained beautiful rosary beads of rock crystal mounted in gold which had been blessed by the Pope.[3]

Lough Conn, another horse named from the Irish landscape, did actually come second to Caughoo at Aintree. Lough Conn was owned by Paddy Rowe who had a small holding of 18 acres in the townland of Longford, Crossmolina, County Mayo, along the shores of Lough Conn. Paddy went to England to work and make some money. While there, Lady Luck smiled on him. Just around the outbreak of the Second World War he won £20,000 on the football pools. Shortly afterwards a headline in a Manchester newspaper stated that 'An Irish Fool wins the Pools.' That statement is reputed to have cost the newspaper £5,000 and left Paddy so much richer. He returned home to Mayo and bought the Knockglass estate which had been owned by the deceased Paget sisters. The estate was heavily timbered. Paddy set up a saw-mill and soon recovered its price.[4]

Paddy had an interest in horse racing too. He bought a tough little horse of about 16 hands. He ploughed him as a $1\frac{1}{2}$ year old, and called him Lough Conn after the lake beside which he was reared. He had him trained by Harry Boland, a member of the Church of Ireland, and also a great rugby player with the Ballina team. Lough Conn first came to public notice when he won three point-to-point races in one day in 1944 at Dooneen outside Enniscrone in County Sligo. That day at Aintree in 1947, the betting on Lough Conn was 33/1. After his defeat in the Grand National, Lough Conn subsequently won the Cunningham Cup in the same year.

I hope this story of a horse race in 1947 is another illustration of how our townlands and names mean things to us. They are places of identification, places of belonging. They help the genealogist monitor the movement of people. When descendants of emigrants return from far off shores trying to trace their roots with only a fragment of a townland name, the genealogist is able to go to a map, identify that place, and then get in touch with parish and other records. The townland is the key to all sorts of stories.

For example, take the families I have mentioned. The McDowells can trace their roots in the parish of Kilmore well back to the eighteenth century and their further origins to the time that Gaelic was spoken in the south of Scotland. The Mayo tradition maintains that the Rowe family, along with the McAnallens, McErlanes, Holmes, Craigs, and others migrated from Armagh to County Mayo in about 1796, after the clash known as the battle of the Diamond in 1795. It is said that some 4,000 people moved to Mayo as a result of the economic and sectarian strife in the densely overpopulated county of Armagh, and that these people had been involved in the Ulster linen industry of the time. Lord Sligo welcomed these immigrants in whom he saw weaving skills which would complement the spinning industry which was well established in County Mayo. As time passed they formed little colonies near Castlebar, Newport, Westport, Ballina and Crossmolina. One observer noted with approval the clicking of the looms in the Barony of Tirawley. At the fairs and markets in Newport these people were known as *Ultaigh* or Ulstermen. So it was in keeping with the tradition from which these families came that Paddy Rowe, with his new found wealth, also invested in a flax scutching mill on the edge of Ballina town in the 1940s. And he afforded himself the luxury of a little horse named after the lake bordering the townland of Longford where his ancestors and others had found a home in 1796, having crossed Lough Conn in wicker boats.

Notes and references

1 The Ordnance Survey spelling of this name is 'Cauhoo'.
2 *General Valuation of Rateable Property in Ireland, Union of Cavan* (Dublin 1857).
3 £1000 in 1947 is roughly equivalent to £25,000 in 2004.

History through drama. Pupils from Scoile Mhuire, Clontibret, County Monaghan performed a drama about 'the hiring fair'. Participants were, Christopher Brennan, Joseph Brennan, Christina Duffy, Niall Duffy, Fergal Greenan, Francie McAtavey, Eoin McGuigan, Tara McKeown, Elaine McNally, Shane McNally, Noelle Marray, Karl Moen, Christopher Morgan, Shane Murphy, Jonathan Rice, David Savage, and Cara Sherlock; teacher, Geraldine Clarke.

Only a sin if you're caught? Cross border smuggling in the Irish Folklore Collection

Emer Ní Cheallaigh

I confess that, coming from the village of Finglas in north-west Dublin, a place with a larger population than Limerick City, I do not have personal experience of 'the heart's townland'. I have had to content myself with sharing in the experiences of others through my collecting work around the country, where I have been welcomed in many places, particularly the twenty-two townlands of the parish of Truagh in Monaghan, and in Killeter and Aghyaran in Tyrone and Carndonagh in Donegal. There I was privileged to experience the genuine feeling of pride, belonging, identity, and community spirit that allowed individuals in these townlands and others to share their stories of smuggling with an outsider.

I don't intend to detail the general history of partition and the creation of the political border between the two states in Ireland. With the help of the archive of the Irish Folklore Commission, now housed in the Department of Irish Folklore at University College, Dublin, I do hope briefly to draw attention to smuggling lore in Ireland, and the effect of smuggling on community attitudes in many townlands around the border.

Before the creation of 'the border', smuggling was generally carried out by sea around the coast of the island of Ireland, particularly by islanders on Tory, Rathlin, Sherkin and Cape Clear and, of course, the large port cities of Dublin, Waterford, Belfast and Cork. Coastal smuggling stories tended to be lengthy and dramatic narratives set on the high seas with contraband and luxury goods such as rum, tobacco, silks and perfumes being 'purchased' from foreign vessels lurking around the Irish coast. In 1940, the folklore collector Michael Corduff described memories of early nineteenth century coastal 'Smuggling Days', in Rossport, County Mayo. Corduff tells us that Seoirse Ó Máille, Paudheen Bán A'Cormack, Duffer Doyle and others were known as 'the kings of contraband traffic'. He continues:

> …the smuggling traffic was vigorously aided and abetted by the coastal natives who acted as coastal sentinels and guides for the smuggling ships in their tortuous passage through hazardous rocks and islands in their evasion of the naval watchdogs of the Crown. [1]

The border which came into effect in the early 1920s created two very different economies and systems of administration. This new land frontier, running for approximately 300 miles, created and fostered small-scale economic instabilities and political and religious hostilities that were felt in the heart of many townlands and which were influential factors in the birth of cross-border smuggling and its related lore.

Smuggling seems to have had an effect on the financial situation of people extending beyond the lower economic classes. This extract from County Louth tells of a small time publican's financial situation before and after he began smuggling.

> Paddy owed the sum of two hundred and fifty pounds to Carolan's of Dundalk, wholesale suppliers of stout and spirits. His pub was small and dilapidated. He wouldn't sell a dozen bottles of stout in a week in the old days…this was before the smuggling started, and he was in debt rings around him.[2]

Once the publican began smuggling, his circumstances changed dramatically. Paddy could use the proceeds of his legitimate goods from Carolan's to clear his debts while still managing to run his business with the profits made from smuggling.

> (His) credit was extended, and with the proceedings of the sales Paddy incurred debts with other travellers and paid them with the money he made off Carolan's stuff. [3]

This differs greatly from individuals smuggling on a large scale, purely for profit. Professional smugglers either made their money from the goods themselves or they were employed as smugglers by other people. A successful smuggler, having made his or her fortune, could retire and employ local individuals to smuggle on their behalf. In 1953, Charlie Douglas from Layd in Antrim informs us that the fee for smuggling tobacco in the leaf was a half a crown a night for a whole night's carrying 'and half a crown was a lot them times.'[4] Despite the harsh penalties if caught, the profits generated by commercial smuggling appear to have made participation in the activity a risk worth taking. Both types of smuggling contributed to the sustenance and development of small rural communities in the physical sense and, consequently, to the sustenance and development of community tradition.

Various methods were used to smuggle these goods over the border. This next extract from the School's Manuscript Collection, tells of a Donegal woman's imaginative method of smuggling in preparation for Christmas.

> A short time after the border was established between Moville and Derry, an old woman wanted to get a turkey across the border, and she did not know how to do it. Then she thought of a plan and this is the plan. She dressed the turkey as a baby and put a long white frock on it and put a bonnet on its head and put a white shawl around it. She then filled a feeding bottle with milk and put it in the turkey's mouth and in this way she got the turkey across the border.[5]

This action definitely proves the theory that necessity is the mother of all invention! Another equally imaginative method of smuggling is described in another story from Birdstown National School in the parish of Fahan Upper, found in the Donegal School's Manuscript Collection.[6]

> A man known as the Boheal [7] was one day smuggling yeast past the customs post so when he came near the border he went into a house, left his yeast and got a cat in the bag. He scared it well up and when he came to the post the

customs man asked him to open the bag against his will and out jumped the cat. The Boheal let on he was angry and followed his cat back to try to catch it. It run the faster. Then he went into the house, and got his yeast in the bag of course. The customs man didn't want to scare his cat again so he got past safe.[8]

In some cases where individuals had properties straddling the border, and could avail of the positive elements of both economies, it was sometimes possible to evade prosecution by moving from one jurisdiction to another - that is, in one door and out the other!

The logistics of cross border smuggling involved a large amount of local knowledge and familiarity with the surrounding townlands. In many of the narratives, community support and co-operation were essential to ensure the success of the mission. The majority of the larger smuggling episodes were conducted by night both by individuals and by bands of smugglers, thus an intimate familiarity with the local terrain was essential. Goods had to be conveyed through stonewalled fields, over streams and through unapproved border crossings, as quickly as possible and without drawing attention. Many possible hiding places were needed and these were often named to reflect their cache, such as 'the Brandy Hole', 'Strapa an Tobac'[9] and 'the Sugary Road'.

This smuggling lore was collected predominantly by the full and part time collectors of the Irish Folklore Commission in the form of descriptive narratives, songs, poems and local legends. Generally the lore relating to cross border smuggling is laced with humour and tends to treat the smuggler as a hero, with a quick wit and imagination, often making a fool out of the authorities. In imaginative appearance, the smugglers tend to be of large stature with prominent features and are capable of amazing feats of strength. One short reference from the schools collection describes two female smugglers from Carndonagh in Donegal:

Her name was Mary Hartin. She would leave home at seven o'clock in the morning and go to Derry and be back in the [evening] at seven. She would carry all her goods home in a sack on her back. There was another woman living in Árd Barrick, her name was Kate McDaid. She would leave home at four o'clock in the morning. She would put a rope in a creel of eggs on her back and carry it to Derry. On her way coming home and going she would knit a pair of socks.[10]

An analysis of the material from the townlands around the border has revealed two distinct types of smuggling and various grades of smugglers. Individuals smuggled to feed their families and to maintain an adequate standard of living, while others earned a small fortune from smuggling. In general, the goods and the quantities of goods that were smuggled by these two types of smugglers were quite different.

Smuggling was and still is a relatively common activity that requires imagination and flexibility. Smugglers have to change with the economic times and have to conjure up various creative ways to travel from locality to locality, from one jurisdiction to the other, avoiding the authorities and constantly adapting their techniques to the terrain and, of course, to the elements.

In general, the community attitude to smuggling in Killeter and Aghyaran in Tyrone, Carndonagh in Donegal and Truagh in Monaghan, was not a negative one. The treatment of smuggling in recent Irish folklore reveals the perception of smuggling as being a necessity, and that the smugglers had 'no choice' but to smuggle. Community support for smuggling may have arisen from the fact that in the short term, townlands and communities benefited from smuggling. Even individuals who did not engage in smuggling were grateful recipients of the goods. One informant from Truagh, when asked how he felt about smuggling replied, 'Smuggling … sure it is only a sin if you get caught!' Another person from a nearby townland in Monaghan described how the proceeds of smuggling financed the roof of a local house, and the wedding of a neighbour paid for with the proceeds of smuggling.[11] Smuggling was perceived as an activity through which people could improve their standard of living and thus their locality. Communities perceived themselves as benefiting from smuggling in practical ways, and it could also be argued that the community co-operation which was necessary brought individuals together in a sense of solidarity under the umbrella of illegal activity. Smuggling generated an energy through which many townlands functioned and developed. Perversely, and viewed from the local perspective, one might even say that the extent to which smuggling was carried out reflected the strength of the townland's heart, as the profits made were reinvested into local business, properties and lifestyles, all of which ensured that this heart continued to beat.

The Irish smuggling tradition embraces the idea of boundaries in both physical and social senses. Cross border smuggling had a significant impact in the popular culture of the townlands and communities where it formed an integral part of daily life in many of the areas around the border. A significant test of its impact is the extent to which the tales of smuggling, with their excitement generated by the combination of secrecy, profit, cunning and illegality, infiltrated the twentieth century oral tradition. I hope that this short contribution has given you a local glimpse of an enduring human phenomenon.

Notes and references

1 IFC (Irish Folklore Commission, Main Manuscript Collection) 1245: 222-223.
2 IFC 1692: 236.
3 IFC 1692: 237.
4 IFC 1361:185. This interview was recorded in 1953 and the presumption is of reference to the nineteenth century.
5 IFC S (Irish Folklore Collection, Schools' Manuscript Collection) 1119B.
6 The Schools Manuscript Collection is the result of an eighteen-month collecting project carried out in the Irish Republic in 1937-1939 by the Irish Folklore Commission, the Department of Education and the Irish National Teachers Organisation.
7 I am uncertain as to the meaning of this nickname but in a recent interview with Customs Officers in Donegal it was used again. It is possible that the individual was a cattle smuggler and that the name contains *Bó*, the Irish word for cow.
8 IFC S 1109B.
9 In this context, the Irish word 'Strapa' to refers to a ledge or step in a cliff face, where the tobacco would be hidden until it was safe to move.
10 IFC S 1116A.
11 Uncatalogued interviews recorded by the author in March 2003 near Emyvale, County Monaghan.

Paying attention. Left, Niamh McGrath; below from left, Myrtle Hill, Tess Maginess, and Stan Brown.

The Northern Ireland Place-Name Project

Patrick McKay

> That peak was the seat of *Boirche*, the cowherd of the son of *Ross Rigbuidhe*. And he would tend every cow equally from Dunseverick to the Boyne, and they would come (at his call) to *Bend Bairche*, and no cow would graze more than another. Whence *Bend Bairche*, 'Boirche's Peak', derives its name.[1]

This quotation, which offers an explanation of the origin of the Irish name for the Mourne Mountains - *Beanna Boirche* - is taken from the *Dindsenchas*, a lengthy medieval literary tract which appears in both prose and verse and consists of the lore of famous places in Ireland. This particular literary *genre* is peculiar to Ireland and while the explanations of the place-names belong to the realm of legend rather than of fact (for instance, *Beanna Boirche* in fact appears to signify 'the cliffs of the peak district' rather than '*Boirche's* Peak'), the very existence of such literature is evidence of a special fascination with place-names and with their origins.

The establishment of the Northern Ireland Place-Name Project in 1987 could be seen as meeting a long-standing need for authoritative information on the meaning and origin of local place-names. While the Ordnance Survey had employed the eminent Irish scholar John O'Donovan to establish the origin of the names of all the townlands of Ireland in the middle of the last century, the results of the survey (recorded on little handwritten books known as the Ordnance Survey Name Books) were never published. Moreover, although O'Donovan had an uncanny instinct for identifying original Irish derivations, he lacked the historical documentation which is available to the modern place-name scholar, and many of his interpretations of local place-names cannot now be regarded as entirely satisfactory. Likewise P W Joyce's monumental work on *The origin and history of Irish names of places* (3 volumes, Dublin 1869-1913), while still the standard reference work on Irish place-names, is often lacking in the kind of detailed local investigation which accurate interpretation of each name requires. Although a number of regional place-name studies have since been published (for example, Moore Munn's *Notes on the Place Names of the Parishes and Townlands of the County of Londonderry* in 1925 and MacAleer's *Townland Names of County Tyrone* in 1936), interpretations of place-names in the past were often based on shaky premises, and there was need for a full-scale authoritative study. Even so, in Northern Ireland the decision to provide government funding for place-names research came late in the day by comparison with the Republic of Ireland where state sponsored place-name research has been ongoing since 1946 when the Irish Place-Names Commission was established.

It was in response to a request to Queen's University, Belfast, from the Department of the Environment for Northern Ireland for a major research project into all the names of settlements and physical features appearing on the

Ordnance Survey 1:50,000 scale map that the Place-Name Project was originally established in 1987. A team of five suitably qualified people was recruited, under the directorship of Professor Stockman of the Department of Celtic, and their brief was to establish the original form and meaning of the place-names and to note any historical or other relevant information. Initially, funding came from the Department of the Environment but in 1990 responsibility was transferred to the Central Community Relations Unit who requested that the results of the research should be published, and that names of all administrative units (including townlands, parishes and baronies) should be included. The result is the first seven volumes in the *Place-Names of Northern Ireland* series, published by the Institute of Irish Studies at Queen's University. Four of these volumes deal with parts of County Down, two with parts of County Antrim and one with County Derry. The launch of each volume has been met with great interest and enthusiasm in the relevant locality and we regularly receive requests for volumes from areas not yet dealt with. The fact that the first three volumes in the series deal with County Down was due to the fact that a certain amount of research on that county had already been carried out by the late Deirdre Flanagan, a former lecturer in the Department of Celtic of Queen's University. However, it was decided that rather than finish the whole county of Down before moving on it would be better to widen the interest of the Project by publishing volumes on other counties. We were also wary of leaving ourselves open to charges of discrimination from those who did not belong to County Down!

The decision to site the Northern Ireland Place-Name Project in the Celtic Department of Queen's University (now Irish and Celtic Studies in the School of Languages, Literatures and Arts) was a recognition of the fact that the majority of the place-names of Northern Ireland are of Irish origin and that their interpretation requires a good knowledge of the Irish language at all stages of its development. However, it must be emphasized that names of Norse, Anglo-Norman, Ulster Scots and English origin are studied with equal care and it is recognized that the cultural landscape has been immeasurably enriched by all of these. The Celtic Department of Queen's University has a distinguished record of place-name research. The aforementioned John O'Donovan, who was regarded as the leading place-names authority of his day, was the first Professor of Celtic in Queen's (1850-61), and in this century three members of staff have been leading authorities on place-names. They were Michael A O'Brien (Professor of Celtic, 1945-47), Seán Mac Airt (Head of Department, 1948-59), and Deirdre Flanagan, Lecturer and later Senior Lecturer (1952-84). From 1990 until his retirement in 1996 the general editor of the Place-Names of Northern Ireland series was the Professor of Celtic, Gerry Stockman. Since then the position has been filled by Dr Nollaig Ó Muraíle, Senior Lecturer in Irish and Celtic, and for many years a Place-Names Officer with the Place-Names Branch of the Dublin Ordnance Survey.

In 1993 the Central Community Relations Unit appointed Professor Bill Nicolaisen, a place-names scholar of international standing, to carry out an evaluation of the Project. In his report he stated:

> There is no onomastic survey in the British Isles which has this kind of modern set-up, and even the renowned and productive name institutes in the Nordic countries (in Copenhagen, Uppsala, Helsinki, Oslo, and Reykjavik, and to a lesser extent in Lund and Gothenburg) and the onomastic centre at the University of Leipzig in the former DDR look rather old-fashioned compared with the Onomastic Project at Queen's. In the last five and a half years, Northern Ireland has acquired a research unit which is truly unique and to which others will look with admiration and envy.

As a result of this report the Central Community Relations Unit reported to the Minister responsible for Community Relations that a centre of excellence had been established, and funding for the project was promised to the end of March 1997. While the award of three years' funding was obviously to be welcomed, the fact that the government had now decided not to renew the funding beyond that time meant that in effect the Project was to be abandoned before it was even half complete.

There followed a lean period of two years during which the Project was left with no core funding, but in the course of which I was fortunate enough to obtain grants from the Community Relations Council and from the Ultach Trust to produce my *Dictionary of Ulster Place-Names* which appeared in 1999. Meanwhile my colleague Kay Muhr worked tirelessly (and without salary) on applications for further funding and managed to achieve a grant from the Arts and Humanities Research Board which commenced in March 1999 and is due to end on 31 March 2004. As a result of this grant the first Armagh and Fermanagh volumes in the *Place-Names of Northern Ireland* series will shortly appear. They are Mícheál Ó Mainnín's volume on Armagh city and district, and my own volume entitled *Lisnaskea and District: the Parish of Aghalurcher*. A Tyrone volume entitled *Dungannon to the Blackwater* is also in preparation but unfortunately the current round of funding does not allow for its publication and instead it has been decided to produce a popular volume on the place-names of the Dungannon District Council area. In 1999, Kay Muhr also obtained a grant from the Heritage Lottery Fund to produce a millennium exhibition entitled 'Celebrating Ulster's Townlands' which has toured widely in Ulster and beyond and has been very well received.

While the *Place-Names of Northern Ireland* series can be regarded as the flagship product of the Project, it is recognised that production of such detailed volumes is both time-consuming and costly. Given that since 1997 the research team has been reduced from five to two, it is not regarded as realistic to seek the long-term funding necessary to complete the entire series, which would run to some forty volumes. However, if local funding can be raised for a book on any particular area we will of course be happy to provide it.

Apart from the *Place-Names of Northern Ireland* series, the Project provides an important service to the public in a number of other ways. Members of the research team are always in demand to respond to public enquiries, to give talks to schools and local historical societies, and to provided advice to district councils on appropriate names for new housing developments. With the change in the law to allow for the erection of bilingual street and road names, the Northern Ireland Place-Name Project is in a unique position to provide reliable and impartial advice as to the most appropriate Irish forms. Under the Good Friday Agreement the Irish language (and also, to some extent, Ulster Scots) has for the first time been given official recognition in Northern Ireland. Many official documents which include place-names are now being translated and reliable Irish forms of the names need to be provided. The Ordnance Survey of Northern Ireland's Pointer Project will restore townlands to all postal addresses (although it is currently proposed also to retain the controversial rural road naming system), and the Northern Ireland Place-Name Project is in a position to provide reliable Irish-language versions of these names.

At the heart of the work of the Northern Ireland Place-Name Project for the past sixteen years has been the creation of a database of historical spellings of the place-names of Northern Ireland. This database is now nearing completion and we believe that it is an extremely valuable resource for a wide range of people, including local historians, archaeologists and genealogists and that it can be of great interest to the general public. We believe that it is vital that it be maintained and made generally accessible as soon as possible.

We envisage a number of 'spin-off' products from the database, some of which are listed below:

- On-line interpretations of place-names based on the historical evidence contained in the database.
- An on-line and published gazetteer of Northern Ireland place-names, to include all the place-names which appear on the Ordnance Survey 6-inch maps.
- An on-line and published bilingual gazetteer of Northern Ireland place-names.
- Educational materials for schools and other institutions.
- Co-operation with the Culture Northern Ireland project in the Nerve Centre in Derry to provide on-line information on place-names.
- In the context of cultural tourism, provision of instant information at tourist sites, and in tourist literature, on the cultural significance of local place-names.
- Co-operation with the Ordnance Survey of Northern Ireland in producing bilingual maps.
- A bibliography of sources and other relevant material.
- A handlist of family names in Northern Ireland place-names.
- Popular books on the place-names of Northern Ireland, perhaps in county volumes.
- Adaptation of the database for website display.

We believe that it should be recognised that:

- The place-names of Northern Ireland are an asset that should be protected and maintained.
- Townlands and their names are unique to this island and should remain part of Northern Ireland's address system.
- Place-names reflect all the languages and cultures that have prevailed in this region. Their meanings reflect our landscape, natural history, archaeology, historical events, people and buildings, families, literature and traditions.

We are convinced that closure of the Northern Ireland Place-Name Project at this time would represent a major loss to the community and a waste of valuable existing resources. We believe that the Northern Ireland government should establish a permanent centre for the recording, study and interpretation of local names.

Reference

1 Stokes, Whitley (ed.), 'The prose tales in the Rennes Dindsenchas', in *Revue Celtique*, vol. xvi, p48 (Paris 1895).

Townland diasporas

Brian Lambkin and Patrick Fitzgerald

'Townland diasporas', looks a bit strange? You may not have seen the two terms together before, but we think that in the next few years 'townland diaspora' studies are likely to catch on, and here we attempt to explain why.

As this conference testifies, the term 'townland' is familiar and well-loved by local historians, but what of 'diaspora'? If the term 'diaspora' still sounds strange in relation to Ireland, it is not for want of effort by President Mary Robinson and her successor, Mary McAleese, to make it familiar. Before the 1990s the 'Irish diaspora' was practically unheard of. Previously we had talked about 'the Irish abroad' but not 'the diaspora'. The first encounter with the notion for many was as recently as 1995 when President Mary Robinson made her speech to the twin houses of the Oireachtas on 'Cherishing the Irish Diaspora'.

At her inauguration in 1991, when Robinson first spoke of the diaspora of seventy million people worldwide who can claim Irish descent, she had envisaged cherishing them in a purely symbolic way. She used the emblem of a light in her window signifying 'the inextinguishable nature of our love and remembrance on this island for those who leave it behind'. In 1995 she still took her central image of the 'diaspora,' or 'The Emigrant Irish', from Eavan Boland's poem:

> Like oil lamps we put them out the back,
> Of our houses, of our minds.[1]

Mary Robinson suggested four main ways in which the homeland might 'value, nurture and support' its diaspora. These were: the way we prepare our young people for emigration; the way we communicate between homeland and diaspora; *the way we deal with our history*; and the exemplary way that we on the island live together. Focusing on the way we deal with our history, she pointed out: 'We cannot have it both ways. We cannot want a complex present and still yearn for a simple past.' Her argument is a powerful one: that studying the Irish diaspora is good for us because it confronts us with our own local complexity:

> If we expect that the mirror held up to us by Irish communities abroad will show
> us a single familiar identity, or a pure strain of Irishness, we will be disappointed.
> We will overlook the fascinating diversity of culture and choice which looks back
> at us. Above all we will miss the chance to have that dialogue with our own
> diversity which this reflection offers us.[2]

Robinson's vision of the Irish diaspora continues to be promoted by President Mary McAleese, who takes every opportunity to value positively the relationship between homeland and diaspora and to develop thinking about it by referring to 'the global Irish family'. In this context we should be clear that by the Irish diaspora is meant not only the 'scattering' of emigrants world-wide but also their descendants who still claim some sense of connection with the peoples of the island of Ireland, including those who describe themselves as British or Ulster Scots. What is of interest to us here is how local historians in Ireland might go about 'cherishing' the 'global Irish family', particularly those who make up the Irish diaspora.

So how do townlands and the diaspora fit together? As far as townland studies are concerned, they are in good shape, following the appearance in 1998 of the seminal work gathered together in two major books: *Townlands in Ulster*, edited by Bill Crawford and Bob Foy, and *Irish Townlands*, edited by Brian Ó Dálaigh, Denis Cronin and Paul Connell.[3] These books should have long-term significance in providing a framework and inspiration for further townland studies.[4]

To what extent then has the new Robinsonian thinking about the Irish diaspora impacted on townland studies - especially since the appearance of Donald Akenson's magisterial *The Irish Diaspora: A Primer?*[5] The short answer is, not greatly. Most townland studies mention emigration. How could they not? But beyond quantifying the numbers who left, and perhaps referring to the destinations to which they went, it is rare for interest to be taken in the continuing relationship between the emigrants and their 'home' townland. One of the best examples known to us of a townland study that takes a closer interest in its emigrants is John Bradley's book on his home place of Gallon in west Tyrone.[6]

In what might be described as 'the Gallon diaspora' we find McLaughlins leaving Gallon for the United States, Canada, England (Huddersfield), Scotland (St Johnstone), Wales and Australia (Sydney); Brogans for Philadelphia; and McGarveys for San Francisco. One of the McAnena's emigrated to Scotland, found work with a farmer in Ayrshire and later on a hydro-electric scheme in the Highlands. Members of the Morris family went as priests and nuns to the United States and England. There is a fine photograph of one of the Quinns, taken the day before she emigrated to Philadelphia. One of the McConnells emigrated to the United States in the 1950s and returned to buy a farm from the Hill family in Gallon. Similarly, one of the Bradleys emigrated to Australia and returned to buy a farm in Gallon.[7]

Gallon also provides an excellent example of how townland studies can develop and travel. *One Lifetime Is Not Enough* is the recently published autobiography of Patrick Kelly, who was born in 1904 in Scotland to parents who were both from Gallon. They brought him back to live in Gallon when he was a few months old. At the age of 20 he emigrated to Australia, returning to Gallon only for a visit in 1978, aged 73:

> My sisters and their families made me very welcome and I met nieces and nephews by the dozen. But of my old schoolmates, about six were left; of course, a few still exist in America, where I have many cousins. [8]

As well as this migration between the townland of Gallon and its diaspora, the book tells of further interaction. Its publisher, Joseph Farrell, who lives in

Colorado, is part of the Gallon diaspora. In the course of doing research about his mother's family, who was a Kelly born in Gallon, he found John Bradley's book about the townland. He contacted Bradley by telephone and eventually visited Gallon where:

> [Bradley] introduced us to many of the people in the townland who knew my mother's family and we also found that a cousin (the existence of whom I knew nothing) was living in the very house where my mother and some of her siblings had been born.[9]

It was on this visit that he was shown the manuscript of the autobiography of his cousin Patrick Kelly. So intrigued was he by it that he visited Patrick Kelly's children in Australia and 'walked in Patrick's footsteps through the countryside, towns and cities of Victoria, Australia as well as in the townlands of Co. Tyrone, Ireland'. So we can see how this story confronts us with our 'local complexity'. The publication *One Lifetime Is Not Enough* is in itself a sign of the ongoing relationship between Gallon and its diaspora.

We can also see from the example of Gallon that the Irish diaspora as a whole can be thought of as an aggregation of thousands of townland diasporas, each with its own story. Of course, as in the case of Gallon, we can break the townland diaspora down into its most fundamental component parts, the migration stories of individual family members that constitute 'family diasporas'. Here it is that family history and local history, townland studies and migration studies come together. It is a rare family tree in Ireland that has no branches abroad. So we may see that a powerful way of cherishing the Irish diaspora would be for the family historian to take a closer interest in the 'family diaspora', and for the local historian to attend to the village, townland, parish, or county diaspora. Among the most poignant expressions of emigrant feeling are the headstones in graveyards around the world that bear the name of an Irish townland, such that in Arrowtown graveyard, South Island, New Zealand, to John McKibbin, 1894, 'native of Marshallstown, Downpatrick, Co. Down, Ireland.'[10]

The emigrants of past centuries may not have articulated their sense of belonging in the terms we use here, but the reading of emigrant letters confirms that emigrants were conscious of family and townland diasporas. Let us consider one emigrant letter from almost 3000 held on the Irish Emigration Database, a virtual archive of digitised sources pertaining to emigration from Ireland to North America 1700-1950, held at the Centre for Migration Studies at the Ulster-American Folk Park, Omagh.

On 4 December 1900 James O'Brien, then living in Montreal, Canada, wrote home to his younger sister, Bella, who remained resident in the townland of Aghnagar, County Tyrone.[11] Just three weeks before Christmas, James began his letter with the central concern of much emigrant correspondence – the remittance. Bella would find enclosed a bank draft for twenty pounds sterling, comprising her usual quarterly allowance of ten pounds supplemented by a further 'Xmas Box' of ten pounds. We can see from this how important the relationship with its emigrants could be to the well-being of the townland.

James then requested that Bella write to him in order to keep him abreast of all the family news. He drew his sister's attention, in particular, to their relations, the Kellys. He reminded her of Father John, a parish priest in England and his brother, Michael who was farming near Keady in county Armagh. Then he recalled another cousin, Father Michael O'Brien, a priest in Loughgall, also in county Armagh, and his two brothers whom he thought were still living in the townland of Sessiadonaghy, between Ballygawley and Dungannon, county Tyrone. This townland bordered his own native townland of Aghnagar from which he had left 'the old homestead'. In this passage of the letter we can see James O'Brien mapping out in his own head, for the benefit of his sister, the Kelly/O'Brien family diaspora.

James then recalled to Bella his last return visit home to Aghnagar, four years previously. He remembered his meeting with John O'Brien 'the only one of the name in my native townland' still remaining. James reflected sadly to his sister 'all were gone except him, I felt sad and lonely when I thought of the numbers, respect and position the family had fifty years ago to that of 1896'.

Keen to keep his mental map up to date, James requested of his sister, '… if you happen to know anything about any of them just let one hear it.'

In essence James O'Brien's plea is not very different from the challenge that we present to local historians here. In researching and writing about your townland, parish, or barony, do not forget and neglect all of those who left and spread across the globe. Apart from anything else, reconnecting your local place with its diaspora today makes good business sense. As John Bradley can vouch, his book on Gallon sold well to its diaspora outside Ireland, so like Bella O'Brien perhaps we could tap in to this potential 'Christmas Box'.

But there are nobler issues at stake here as well. To take account of the migration dimension of family and community history is to connect with the wider world; to see the local 'home' place in its regional, national and international context, and, as Mary Robinson put it, to 'confront our local complexity'. It is also a practical way of 'cherishing' the Irish diaspora. Townland studies are burgeoning. A recent example is the splendid study of Portavo, County Down by Peter Carr.[12] Irish migration studies are also growing, as Kevin Kenny's recent overview demonstrates.[13] It is only a matter of time, we think, before the words 'townland' and 'diaspora' no longer seem strange together, and all involved in family and local history are familiar with 'townland diasporas'.

Notes and references

1 Eavan Boland, 'The Emigrant Irish', in *Outside History: Selected Poems 1980-1990* (New York 1987).

2 'Cherishing the Irish Diaspora', Address to the Houses of the Oireachtas by President Mary Robinson on a Matter of Public Importance, 2 February 1995.

3 W H Crawford and R H Foy (eds), *Townlands in Ulster: Local History Studies* (Belfast 1998); Brian Ó Dálaigh, Denis A Cronin & Paul Connell, (eds), *Irish Townlands: Studies in Local History* (Dublin 1998).

4 This importance has been discussed by Brian Lambkin in, 'Taking Townland Studies into the New Millennium', *Familia: Ulster Genealogical Review*, Number 14, (Belfast 1998), pp96-107.

5 D H Akenson, *The Irish Diaspora: A Primer* (Belfast 1992, hardback; 1996, paperback).

6 William John Bradley, (2000), *Gallon: the history of three townlands in County Tyrone from the earliest times to the present day* (Derry 2000). See also 'Gallon, County Tyrone' in Crawford and Foy, op. cit., pp155-188.

7 Crawford and Foy, *op. cit.*, pp166-8; Bradley, *op. cit.*, pp99-102.

8 Patrick Kelly, *One lifetime is not enough* (Grand Junction, Colorado 2002), p240.

9 *Ibid.*, p13.

10 M K Muhr, *Celebrating Ulster's Townlands* (Belfast 2000).

11 Centre for Migration Studies reference IED 9004034, copied from PRONI T 1876/2.

12 Peter Carr, *Portavo: an Irish townland and its peoples* (Belfast 2003).

13 Kevin Kenny, 'Diaspora and Comparison: The Global Irish as a Case Study', *Journal of American History*, no. 1, June 2003, pp134-162.

Townlands and the local historian

Jack Johnston

This paper is based on my own practical experience of using townlands in local history, and I want to look at some of the methods of using them to organise local source material. I also want to observe how durable the townland has been for the local historian over the last 400 years.

There has recently been a lot published on the theory and methodology of townland studies in Ulster. Much of the work has been promoted by the Federation for Ulster Local Studies which published Bill MacAfee's first worksheet on how to study a townland as far back 1976, in the third issue of *Ulster Local Studies*.[1] In 1991 the Federation produced *Every stoney acre has a name* which was a most informed celebration of the townland in Ulster.[2] The culmination of the Federation's work came just five years ago when *Townlands in Ulster* was published.[3] It was edited by Bill Crawford and Bob Foy and had contributions from many of the leading practitioners in townland studies. John Bradley, one of the contributors, later expanded his chapter into a separate book on a group of three townlands in County Tyrone.[4] Arguably the best single article on townland studies in any of the leading local journals is Maura Nallen's work on eight townlands near Killeshandra in the 1999 *Breifne* journal.[5] South Ulster also has one of the best sources on townland studies in Paddy Duffy's monumental atlas of the Diocese of Clogher.[6] His chapter on 'The making of the Cavan landscape' in the volume of Cavan essays published shortly afterwards (1995) also takes the townland into the realm of a disciplined study of 'localness'.[7]

The definitive reference work for locating townlands is the alphabetical index based on the Census of Ireland for 1851, which has recently been re-published, and reprinted several times, by the Genealogical Publishing Company of Baltimore.[8] Here every one of the, over 60,000, townlands in the country is listed alphabetically and placed in the context of its parish, barony, poor law union and county. The list gives the acreage of each townland together with the numbers of the Ordnance Survey map sheets where it is to be found. The only administrative unit omitted by the list is the district electoral division (DED), an area which since 1973 has become obsolete in the six counties that make up Northern Ireland.

The townland is the base on which local historians work and is effectively the building block of their trade. This is not just confined to the history of parishes and rural communities but is equally important in the study of our country towns. These are, of course, all built in townlands, so that any study of, say, Monaghan, Cavan or Enniskillen needs an analysis of Roosky, Tirkeenan, Kinnypottle, Swellan, Tonystick or Cornagrade. The townland is the base line on the drawing board.

The majority of our townlands were named before the seventeenth century,

No. of Sheet of the Ordnance Survey Maps.	Names of Townlands and Towns.	Area in Statute Acres.			County.	Barony.	Parish.	County District.	District Electoral D	
		A.	R.	P.					Name.	
140	Foilnamuck .	378	2	19	Cork, W.R. :	Carbery W. (W.D.)	Skull . .	Skull . .	Ballydehob	.
27, 33	Foilnamuck .	389	3	4	Tipperary, N.R.	Ormond Upper .	Dolla . .	Nenagh .	Dolla .	.
13, 21	Foilogohig .	735	2	5	Cork, E.R. .	Duhallow .	Kilmeen .	Kanturk .	Meens	.
17, 18	Foilrim . .	143	1	35	Clare . .	Inchiquin . .	Ruan . .	Corrofin . .	Muckanagh	.
8, 16	Foilycleara . .	408	0	34	Limerick .	Coonagh . .	Doon . .	Tipperary No. 2	Bilboa	.
44, 45	Foilycleary .	341	3	19	Tipperary, S.R.	Kilnamanagh Up.	Doon . .	Tipperary No. 1	Glengar	.
16, 20	Foley . .	383	1	16	Armagh . .	Fews Lower . .	Lisnadill .	Armagh . .	Lisnadill .	.
44, 50	Folistown .	196	2	2	Meath . .	Dunboyne . .	Dunboyne .	Dunshaughlin .	Dunboyne	
1, 2, 4, 5	Folkstown Great or Clonard .	370	3	15	} Dublin	Balrothery East .	Balrothery .	Balrothery	{ Balbriggan, Rural	.
4, 5	Folkstown Little .	124	2	12					(	
25, 26, 31, 32	Follistown .	653	0	33	Meath . .	Skreen . .	Follistown .	Navan . .	Ardmulchan	.
35	Follum Big .	155	3	36	} Fermanagh .	Clankelly . .	Clones . .	Clones No. 2 .	Drestornan	
35	Follum Little	109	2	22						
6, 7	Folly . .	228	2	25	Dublin .	Balrothery West .	Palmerstown .	Balrothery .	Clonmethan	.
34, 35	Fomerla . .	307	0	25	Clare . .	Tulla Upper .	Tulla . .	Tulla . .	Ciooney .	.
7, 12	Fonthill . .	156	1	31	Carlow . .	Idrona West .	Cloydagh .	Carlow No. 1 .	Clogrenan	.
17	Fonthill . .	99	1	13	Dublin . . .	Uppercross .	Palmerston .	Dublin South .	Palmerston	.
31	Fontstown Lower	352	0	5	} Kildare	{ Narragh and Re- } ban East {	Fontstown .	Athy No. 1 .	Fontstown	.
31	Fontstown Upper	326	2	9						
55, 56	Foohagh . .	310	3	26	Clare . .	Moyarta . .	Kilfearagh .	Kilrush . .	Kilkee	.
117	Foolagh . .	106	2	26	Galway . .	Longford .	Tynagh .	Portumna .	Pallas	.

Extract from The General Alphabetical Index to the Townlands ... of Ireland.

although it was not until the coming of the first Ordnance Survey maps in the 1830s that their boundaries were finally settled. They were basic divisions of recorded land ownership and their integrity was reinforced by various surveys and estate maps as the seventeenth and eighteenth centuries progressed. They were used to list the various plantation grants issued to the new colonists after 1610. The new order was conceived in precincts and manors within each planted county. A precinct was equated with a barony while the manors within it were composed of groups of fifteen to twenty townlands on average.

In the grant of King James I to Sir William Parsons for Manor Cecil near Augher in Tyrone we can recognise two thirds or more of the names recited as modern-day townlands.

> Grant to *William Parsons*, of the city of Dublin, Esq. The small proportion of *Ballaclogh* , containing the precinct [parcel] of land called Ballaclogh, otherwise Ballinclogh, and the lands of Sheancarragh, Tawlaght-Ibrony, Killnekiry, and Balitiny, each being one balliboe; Tullafoile, one and $^1/_3$ balliboe; Mullaneighane, Glan-Igeragh, Corcullen, Knocknamany, Cormore, Cloneblaagh, Doongower, Ballyaghenewe, Cloncoose, Ardnuchine, and Lisleagh, one balliboe each; and Cossioghrough, $^1/_3$ of a balliboe; in all, 1,000 acres. The premises are created into the manor of Cecill, with 300 acres in demesne, and a court baron. Rent, 5l. 6s. 8d. English. To hold forever, as of the castle of Dublin, in free and common socage by fealty only, and subject to the conditions of the plantation of Ulster. 12 January, 8th [1610-1611].[9]

If we use lists such as these in conjunction with early maps it is sometimes possible to get a very clear picture of our locality in the early seventeenth century. Most particularly, for counties Armagh, Cavan, Fermanagh and Tyrone the 'Maps of the Escheated Counties', drawn up under Sir Josias Bodley in 1609, can be used. The Bodley maps were far from accurate in terms of acreage or boundaries, but they were a first attempt to set the townlands in their spatial and contiguous positions.[10]

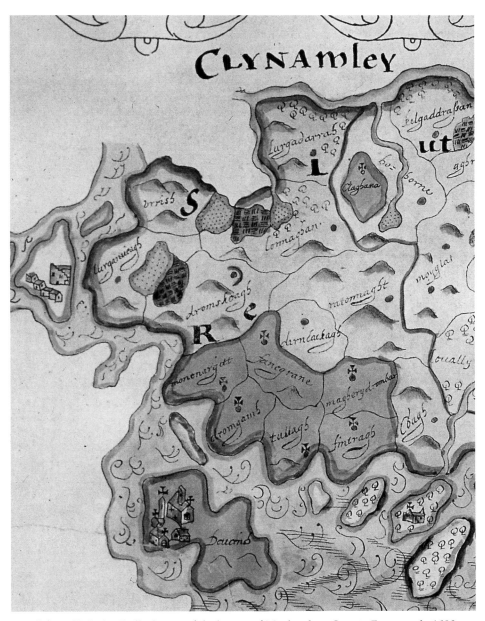

Detail from Sir Josias Bodley's map of the barony of Magheraboy, County Fermanagh, 1609. The island town and castle of Enniskillen are shown on the left, with Devinish and its monastery at the bottom.

The townlands were used to list the estates of the landowners in Sir William Petty's census of 1654-56 -where the record has survived - as well as the 'census' of 1659 subsequently edited by Seamus Pender.[11] They were becoming an important cadastral unit for central administration by the middle of the seventeenth century and were used in the collection of the Hearth Tax in 1665-66.[12] In all these records the majority of the names listed are fairly easily recognised as present-day townlands. The Down Survey made at this time saw many of the townlands listed also placed on maps. Its parish maps were more accurate than anything done before.[13]

In the eighteenth century townlands were the essential units for creating the estate rentals of the landlords. This was when many of them were mapped accurately for the first time. Local historians owe a great debt to the estate mapmakers of the eighteenth century. People like Nicholas Willoughby, John Piers, James Leonard and James Ashmur Junior working here on the estates of south Ulster have left us an invaluable record of our townlands several decades before the Ordnance Survey.[14]

The management and organisation of a large estate relied heavily on the townland as a workable division of landholding. In the early and middle eighteenth century many estates were set by the townland with one man normally responsible for the rent. It was a manageable unit and made rent collection much easier, especially for an absentee owner. In the 1751 Rental of the Blessingbourne estate at Fivemiletown, the landlord, Margetson Armar, then of Castlecoole, was quite content to have contact simply with a head tenant or middleman who, as later evidence shows, had a whole pyramid of occupiers underneath him.

Extract from Blessingbourne estate rental, 1751.

The recurring rentals of all the estates are set up using the townland as the unit for collecting the annual rents. The leases issued to the tenants also make use of the townland in describing the property they hold. This is why the Irish Registry of Deeds, begun in 1708, is such a valuable and still underused archive for local historians. It is accessed under two indexes: firstly, that of the Grantor, but also and more usefully that of place. Here the townlands listed alphabetically for each county provide the entry to any search being made. The Registry in Henrietta Street in Dublin was logistically a difficult place to work in, with large heavy volumes on vellum as the source. The Deeds have now been microfilmed and are easily available now through the Public Record Office in Belfast, although they are a little bit harder to read on the film, especially where the penmanship had faded.

Townlands and local government

It was in the mid and late nineteenth century that the townlands had their maximum administrative use. The new Poor Law of the 1830s defined its 163 Unions by townlands. They were grouped into parishes and then into unions of parishes to support a workhouse, hence the term 'Union'. It was the Poor Law which created the now forgotten District Electoral Divisions (DEDs). They were groups of townlands put together to create electoral units for returning the Board of Guardians.

The new Unions were asked to strike a rate to administer poor relief and to run the workhouse. The first rate books of these Unions date from about 1840, but few survive. However it was from this system that the now familiar printed volumes of Griffith's Second Valuation evolved.[15] Here each occupier is listed by his or her townland with a reference number to correspond to an accompanying map.

Griffith's Valuation with the accompanying maps have become a prime source for local history groups. The revisions of Griffith, known generally as 'the Cancelled Valuations' have enabled detailed analyses of townland history for many people. These revised valuations, classified by their townlands within their DEDs, provide a mass of detail on land ownership, and on the families that worked the land. The cancelled markings – normally at annual or biannual intervals and using different coloured inks – enable a detailed record of townland history to be constructed. This source is useful in tracing farm succession and farm aggrandisment as the nineteenth century progresses. New houses or old ones being raised and slated can often be dated from this record.[16]

The population census, after 1841, was organised under townlands so that by the middle of the century they were an indispensable unit in the local government system. The returns of the 1901 Census were originally tied up in bundles of townlands according to their DEDs and were available in this manner to the local historian in the old Public Record Office at the Four Courts in Dublin. The census is of course now readily available on microfilm but it has been filmed in townland order and in alphabetical order within each DED. Each

COUNTY OF TYRONE.] CENSUS OF IRELAND FOR THE YEAR 1881.

TABLE VII.—AREA, HOUSES, OUT-OFFICES and FARM-STEADINGS, and POPULATION, together with the Valuation of each Parish, TOWNLAND, and TOWNSHIP of the County of TYRONE in 1881

NOTE:—Under the designation "Town" in this table are included all groups of 20 inhabited houses and upwards.

Baronies, Parishes, Townlands, and Towns.	Area in 1881. A. R. P.	Houses 1841.	1851.	1861.	1871.	1881. Total.	In-habited	Unin-habited	Build-ing	Out-offices and Farm-stead-ings.	Population 1841.	1851.	1861.	1871.	1881. Per-sons.	Males.	Fem.	Valuation of Houses and Land in 1881. £ s. d.
CLOGHER BARONY. AGHALURCHER PAR., pt. of: (a)																		
Alderwood, Townland,	838 1 16	15	14	19	19	17	16	1		34	91	92	117	110	94	49	45	125 10 0
Articlea "	334 3 11	23	19	20	17	18	18			71	167	107	100	89	93	44	49	198 5 0
Bogh "	109 1 20	5	7	7	5	5	5			22	35	36	29	27	27	16	11	60 10 0
Brenkly "	111 1 1	6	6	4	5	4	4			12	29	25	17	27	22	11	11	95 0 0
Crockaoleaven "	659 2 30	25	23	19	20	19	19			65	119	122	101	98	94	43	51	116 10 0
Crockanhull "	87 1 37	8	2	2	2	2	2			9	17	20	12	12	14	6	8	22 5 0
Cullentra "	242 0 17	8	8	8	7	6	6			25	54	40	37	33	30	15	15	113 15 0
Cullynane "	129 0 24	8	8	7	6	7	7			34	60	40	32	30	38	21	17	101 5 0
Kill "	652 2 31	29	19	18	20	15	14	1		52	173	88	86	79	70	32	38	183 15 0
Kiltermon "	118 2 23	10	13	12	9	8	8			21	103	62	48	43	24	14	10	87 10 0
Loughermore Glebe "	68 1 5	6	5	5	3	3	3			15	26	22	23	16	13	4	9	40 5 0
Mullaghmore "	266 3 14	17	14	12	13	9	9			57	112	102	63	53	46	21	25	183 5 0
Rahack Glebe "	195 1 7	8	7	5	4	4	4			20	40	30	22	23	28	14	14	69 5 0
Relossy "	354 2 25	11	11	10	7	6	6			21	68	65	47	33	26	12	14	103 5 0
Tattanellan "	111 2 14	7	4	7	6	4	4			13	34	37	34	26	25	12	13	68 10 0
Timpany "	249 3 20	17	13	11	9	9	9			48	100	77	57	50	45	24	21	170 5 0
Tircar "	170 1 7	11	9	9	7	7	7			35	67	55	46	42	40	21	19	111 0 0
Total,	4,708 1 31	222	184	175	169	143	141	2		554	1,304	1,015	871	796	729	350	379	1,850 0 0

The published Census of 1881 not only gave details for that year, but also comparisons with previous censuses.

successive census was then taken with the townland as the unit, until 1971 in Northern Ireland. This provided information for a whole range of statistics, not just on people but on their housing as well. It has made demographic studies possible down to very precise levels. Each published Census after 1851 offered a comparison with its predecessor, and the 1881 Census provided such a comparison over a 40 year spread.

Now, at the beginning of the twenty-first century, we only have census figures for modern wards with shifting boundaries, and even many of the smaller towns and villages are subsumed within these larger units. It is most difficult today, for example, to find population figures not only for single townlands but for small towns like Maguiresbridge or Tempo. The break with the townland as a unit for counting the population in the last three censuses has led to a collapse in the usefulness of the statistics for the purpose of historical comparison.

Townlands and the church

Townlands have been recognised as an indispensable unit by the churches, not only for strictly religious purposes but, for example, in the period when the Church of Ireland parish had local government functions. For example, in the early eighteenth century the parish vestries provided for the upkeep of roads by imposing levies on the townlands through which the roads passed. The inhabitants of particular townlands were employed in repairing roads under nominated overseers. This was the system until 1763 when the responsibility for roadmaking was transferred to the County Grand Juries. In October 1728 the Vestry Book of Clogher parish in County Tyrone records such work:

> … the inhabitants of the Town Lands of Slatmore, Slatbeg, Clogher Anagh, Ballagh, Crossowen, the two Drumhirks, Tullivernan, Aghadrummin, Ratory, Corrick and Farnetra be imployed in repairing the road from Clogher to Ballimagowan bridge and from Clogher to Farnetra bridge and that Mr William Dickson and Mr Thomas Story be overseers.[17]

The Church of Ireland, as the established church, employed the townland as the unit for collecting the tithe. Where these tithe lists survive, they record the tithe paid by each occupier of land, townland by townland. They have now become an invaluable starting point for genealogists in satisfying the roots hunters. It should be said that direct comparisons between these lists and the more widely-known Griffith Valuation need to take into account that the tithes are based on Irish acres. The rate books of the 1840s and the printed Valuation are in statute or English acres. 161 Statute acres are equivalent to 100 Irish or plantation acres.

The townland is vital to Irish genealogists. It has helps us to locate rural people far more easily than anywhere else in the British Isles. I was recently looking through the published Swanzy Will abstracts[18] and was impressed with how, even in the seventeenth century, families were accurately placed because the townland was used in the will. Arthur Forster of Drumgoone in the parish of Aghalurcher left a will dated 1686, William Elliott of Rathmoran left one dated 1696 and John Beatty of Farranseer in the parish of Killeshandra left one dated 1681. In England these men would most probably have been described as 'of the parish of ....'.

Presbyterian and Methodist registers often made full use of the townlands in identifying the parties concerned. This marriage entry in 1835 demonstrates the point:

> John Simpson of Millview in the parish of Aghalow son of the late Thomas Simpson and Anne Burnside his wife of Bloomhill in the parish of Errigal was marryed to Lydia Thompson of Lungs in this parish (Clogher) daughter of the late Robert Thompson and Anne Millar his wife of Bushford in the county of Monaghan.[19]

The townland is of immense value where the search is for a surname which is particularly common in the area. Just imagine trying to disentangle all the McElroys or McGirrs or Johnstons or Hacketts in parts of the Clogher valley if we did not have that extra bit of vital information to hand.

The non-conformist churches had a great affinity with townlands - perhaps it was the anti-parish feeling that they used to distance themselves from the established Church. This is particularly true of the evangelical Protestant movement which flourished in tent meetings or small iron halls throughout the countryside. In my own area it was the 'Killyfaddy meetin' or Clarmore or Dromore 'hall' that satisfied this need. These tiny halls proudly displayed their townland name and with it often the purpose for which they were built.[20]

Gospel Hall, County Down.

Townlands in commerce, education and social life

Shopkeepers also made use of the townland to identify their customers when it came to sending out their accounts. I use the example of a County Tyrone shop ledger from about 1908 which has customers indexed roughly in alphabetical order but with their townland as the defining element. The

Extract from Alexander Steen's shop ledger, c.1908.

Hacketts are strong in the Augher district of south Tyrone and, in the extract illustrated, there are two Andrews, three Pats and three Francis's. Alexander Steen (whose ledger this is) knew them spatially as Andrew of Eskernabrogue and Andrew of the Tramway (a level-crossing cottage), or Francis of Aghamilkin, Francis of Cloneblaugh and Francis of Cullamore – whom some of you may know as Francie Peggy. The little lough at the Border – Francie Peggy's lough – was well known to smugglers on both sides. I must say I also found this ledger a great resource in researching the nicknames in use a hundred years ago. The descendants of the Owen Hackett listed here are the present Pat Owney Barneys. You can also see from it where people are hired – John Hall of Ballagh is hired with Jimmy Trimble.

The National School registers also depended on the townland as a means of identifying families. In fact it was a more important element to them than the father's name. The register of a hundred years ago from a small mountain school in Mullanvaum, near Brookeborough in Fermanagh, could be used to make the point. Boys from the same townland, like the Andersons of Altawalk, may be brothers, but the Goodwins coming from the different townlands of Altaponer and Stripe are unlikely to be so. A register such as this is useful in plotting the school's catchment area by the townlands listed. It also provides us with a socio-economic picture of the families in the area by listing the fathers' occupations. In the case of Mullanvaum school in 1900 it was in an area of small mountain farms, but also an area where herds (or hurds) were used to caretake farms for more prosperous infield farmers.

The Orange Order also displays many townland names through nameboards and signs on their rural halls, although today many of these names have been removed for security reasons - places like Loughans, Dergina, the Bawn, Aughintober and Mulnahunch in Tyrone, or Corlatt, Mullahara and Ballinagall in Monaghan, or Billis, Rathkenny or Corlugan in Cavan. The vast majority of rural lodges take their name from the townland where they meet. In comparison it is worth pointing out that the Gaelic Athletic Association was mainly developed at parish level so that the townland has not become an integral part of its nomenclature. The GAA has, on the other hand, been one of the chief promoters of our consciousness of 'county', that 400-year-old English innovation in Ireland.

Townlands on maps and other paper, and on stone

The Ordnance Survey map sheets are, of course, a prime source for townland history. The initial six-inch to the mile series of the 1830s and its first revision from 1845 onwards fixed our townland boundaries more or less for all time. They were exceptionally accurate documents and recorded a wide range of detail – field boundaries from 1845, houses, mills, churches, schools, wells, watercourses, roads, quarries, sand pits and historic monuments. Never start to research a townland without looking at the past and present Ordnance Survey maps.

I summarise by giving an example of documentary material existing, in addition to Ordnance Survey maps, for a single townland in County Tyrone:

TIMPANY, 248 acres.

Parish of Aghalurcher; DED of Fivemiletown; Barony of Clogher;

Poor Law Union of Clogher; Estate of Blessingbourne (Montgomery).

1752	Rental of Blessingbourne Estate, (1 tenant named).
1775	Map of the townland by James McGirr, (6 tenants named).
1789	Survey and Rental of estate.
1798	Rental of estate, (6 tenants named).
1810	Map of townland (Montgomery estate).
1828	Tithe book for Parish of Aghalurcher.
1843	Agent's Field Book with observations on tenants.
1844	Map of townland with tenant's names.
1860	Griffith's Valuation.
1861–1930	Cancelled Valuation books.
c1890–1918	Register of Andrews Wood National School.
1901	Census.
1911	Census.

The 1843 Field Book listed above is a marvellous source – a mixture of the 1841 Census with details on the leases and the lives still in being, as well as listing the undertenants. The comments include mention of those who have emigrated, non-residents, rich and poor. Often the name is crossed out and the new tenant's name written in, obviously in a later hand.

Finally it should be said that many people took their townlands with them to the grave. The vast majority of headstones in rural Ulster in the nineteenth century and through the twentieth recite the townland of the deceased. It was almost as important as the surname. This was vital too where the same surname proliferated. If you walk through Cappagh graveyard near Omagh where the Grahams and McFarlands are numerous it is important to know if you are a McFarland of Crosh or Fecarry or Lislap. Similarly in the Aughnacloy district it is important to know which Hagan or Quinn you are looking for.

In some cases you will simply see a low modern headstone with two words on it – the surname and the townland, like 'Hall, Tiercar' or 'Mayne, Recolpa'. If it is a small townland which nowadays has become a single farm you can easily see how the townland name would become synonymous with the family living there.

Dr Dallat, elsewhere in this volume, has already chronicled the Ulster local history movement's 'Save our townlands' campaign. It demonstrates how it is possible for us to lose, or to retain, important elements of our culture in quite

**86 LISCLARE ROAD,
STEWARTSTOWN, CO. TYRONE**
DISPERSAL SALE
**OF DRUMGORMAL HOLSTEINS
100 COWS AND HEIFERS**

**FRIDAY 18TH OCTOBER
ON THE FARM - COMMENCING AT 11.30 AM**

THE 'CLEEN' HERD
PRODUCTION SALE OF 60 TOP HOLSTEIN

Thursday 24th October at 12 noon
in Dungannon Farmers' Mart

simple ways. For example, I looked at the 1972 Northern Ireland Telephone directory. There were lots of people called Watt living around Donaghmore and Pomeroy. They are almost all farming families – dispersed in Coolmaghery, Kerrib, Corkhill, Drumhirk, Drummond and Munderadoe. Their stories can be traced through the various townland sources over at least two hundred years. But consider how we find the same people in the present, at various numbers on Cappagh Road, Aghintober Road and Gortnagola Road. This utterly confusing move away from the townlands, if it is not reversed, will have sad and far-reaching consequences.

Consider, finally, auctioneers' advertisements. Some farms no longer proclaim their spatial integrity and are now scaled down to places like 86 Lisclare Road or 19 Islandhill Road. Perhaps animals are more secure than people, as they retain their identity as the Cleen Herd or the Drumgormal Holsteins!

Notes and references

1 W MacAfee, 'The study of the history of a townland – a worksheet', in *Ulster Local Studies*, vol. 2, no. 1, (1976).

2 Tony Canavan (ed.), *Every stoney acre has a name* (Belfast 1991).

3 W H Crawford & R H Foy (eds.), *Townlands in Ulster* (Belfast 1998).

4 William John Bradley, *Gallon: the history of three townlands in County Tyrone from the earliest times to the present day* (Derry 2000).

5 Maura Nallen, 'A study of eight townlands in the parish of Killeshandra, 1608-1841' in Breifne, IX, no. 35 (1999), pp5-84.

6 Patrick J Duffy, *Landscapes of South Ulster: A Parish Atlas of the Diocese of Clogher* (Belfast 1993).

7 Raymond Gillespie (ed.), *Cavan: Essays on the History of an Irish County* (Dublin 1995).

8 *General Alphabetical Index to the Townlands and Towns, Parishes and Baronies of Ireland* (Baltimore, USA, 2000).

9 Printed in Rev George Hill, *An historical account of the Plantation of Ulster* (Belfast 1877; republished Shannon 1970), p267.

10 The Bodley maps are available in the Public Record Office of Northern Ireland under T/2543/24 and T/1965/2D.

11 Seamus Pender, *A Census of Ireland, circa 1659* (Dublin 1939).

12 A cadastral unit is one surveyed at a large enough scale to show its extent and measurement, for purposes such as the identification of ownership or liability for taxation..

13 Down Survey maps 1654-56 (PRONI T/2313). Facsimiles of the maps are also available through the library service.

14 For the definitive work see J H Andrews, *Plantation Acres – An historical study of the Irish land surveyor* (Belfast 1985).

15 Griffith's *Valuation* can be consulted at record offices or through the library service. See also Griffith's *Valuation* published by Eneclann in Dublin: http://www.irishorigins.com/ .

16 The Cancelled Valuation Books for Northern Ireland, covering the period from 1858 to 1929, are available in the Public Record Office of Northern Ireland in Belfast, indexed under Val 12B, with the relevant maps held under Val 2D. Those for the Irish Republic, also with the relevant maps, are now held in the valuation Office at the Irish Life Centre, Abbey Street Lower, Dublin.

17 Clogher Parish Vestry Book 1713-1795. (PRONI MIC/1/22).

18 Clifford, Andrew J, 'Swanzy Will Abstracts [including Index]' in *Irish Genealogist*, 9, no. 4 (1997), pp441-93.

19 Clogher Presbyterian Marriage Register, 1 May 1835. (PRONI MIC/1P/96).

20 Francis X McCorry in his delightful book *Journeys in County Armagh* and *Adjoining Districts* (Lurgan 2000), with its sub-title, *An Exploration of Landscape, Population, Worship and Diversity*, has examined this aspect of religious identity very thoroughly.

The graveyard shift

John B Cunningham

A graveyard can be read, just like any other part of the landscape. The information is there when we become aware of what we should be looking for. In graveyards there are boundaries, divisions, and accents on place and location which we can often miss. This short contribution points out some of these social, religious, financial and geographical boundaries.

The names on the headstones reflect the people who have lived in this particular locality in the past, so if you find a lot of Maguire names in a graveyard you are probably in Fermanagh where the Maguires were chieftains for hundreds of years. Likewise for the name Johnston in Fermanagh where this name is the second most common name after the ubiquitous Maguires.[1] Similarly we get numerous O'Reillys in Cavan graveyards, O'Donnells in Donegal graveyards, and regional variations in all areas. Thus in the small area around Belleek and Garrison in Fermanagh you will find a lot of Keowns, reflecting the local strength of that family in that area.

Most graveyards were not formally enclosed until an act of Parliament in 1866 and the minimum area was normally enclosed on account of cost.[2] So at older burial sites there may be many burials in the surrounding fields. This Act also stipulated that people should be buried in a grave six feet deep and three feet wide, as much shallower burials had been common, and dependent on the energy of the gravedigger and how much he was paid. Ancient graveyards can be several metres above the adjacent land because of the number of bodies buried there. Large and important sites like Clogher Cathedral Graveyard in Tyrone, which has been in use for about 1600 years, must contain many, many thousands of burials.[3]

People had to pay, and still have to pay, for a burial plot in the graveyard and particular locations may have been preferred. Since it was expected that the Resurrection at the end of time would be manifest from the south-east, from the direction of the Holy Land, this was the preferred part of the graveyard for burial. It follows that the north-west was the least preferred. Burial near the grave of a saint had an even higher rating – resurrection by association! Burial inside the church was also much sought after and consequently more expensive. In the seventeenth century the Vestry Minutes of what is now St Macartan's Cathedral in Enniskillen show that it cost sixpence to be buried in the graveyard but £1 inside the building – a forty-fold differential.[4] Vaults are now considered a health risk and most are permanently closed but these are another feature of old graveyards and indicate the wealth and status of the occupants. Cholera and famine pits can also be a feature of some graveyards. Quicklime was frequently used to hasten decomposition.

There were often separate graveyards for unbaptised infants who were not allowed to be buried in consecrated ground, to which Pat Loughrey has referred elsewhere in this volume. People who committed suicide were equally barred, and sometimes buried at a crossroads so as to confuse the errant spirit should it rise and, because of the place of burial, be unable to find its way back to its earthly location.

Different types of division reflect the peculiarities of our society. Often the incoming families of the seventeenth century Plantation used the existing cemeteries and you can find Catholic burials on one side of the graveyard and Protestant burials on the other, as in Carne graveyard near Pettigo, County Donegal. There are also graveyards where related families are buried close together and form a tribal resting place in the cemetery, reflecting their relationships when they were alive. Apparently a form of marriage proposal in our part of the country at one time was the unsubtle question, 'Would you like to be buried with our wans?'

Another geographical divide I found is where people from a certain location bury in the area of the graveyard closest to where they come from. I came upon this in Lettercrann Graveyard, again near Pettigo. Three counties and three parishes meet nearby and those from nearby Tyrone bury in the corner of the graveyard closest to their homes. I had a mental preparation for this discovery when once I was looking at an old photograph of a packed Fair Day in Belleek with a local farmer with an interest in history. He said to me:

> You would think looking at that picture that it is scene of chaos; cattle and people milling here and there with no organisation. On the contrary, the bottom right hand side of the street is where the men from Garrison and the Shore road sell; on the bottom left of the street are the men from Corlea and the Ballyshannon road, and on both sides from half-way up the street are the men from Mulleek. And those boundaries are as rigid as if they were stone walls topped with barbed wire. No Mulleek man would try to sell his cattle among the Garrison men. What would happen if he got into a row? He would have no backings, nobody to help him out or take his part – so everybody stays in their own section of the fair.

So you can draw boundary lines in a Fair Day picture, and in some graveyards there are similar invisible lines.

Identity and place in life can also be seen on headstones. It is usually Roman Catholic graves which are identifiable from the letters IHS – Latin, *Iesus Hominem Salvator*, 'Jesus Saviour of Mankind' - inscribed on them. Few Protestant headstones bear a cross. Other information on a headstone may be in the form of a coat-of-arms, a Masonic symbol, or a symbol of an occupation, e.g. a blacksmith's hammer or anvil. There may be indications that the stone was erected by relatives who had emigrated and done so well that they could afford a fine stone. Typically these were erected by emigrant children over their parents, with an inscription such as 'Erected by their sons and daughters in Philadelphia', reflecting another spatial divide and a social statement by people who had prospered over the seas.

Graveyards close to the sea were often said to have ghosts and eerie noises and were considered dangerous places to be at night. This helped smugglers of silk, tobacco, brandy and wine to use the graveyard as a safe storage place.

Paramilitary organisations have been known to do the same in much more recent times. Body snatchers or 'Sack 'em Ups' stole bodies for doctors and surgeons to practice upon. Burke and Hare were Irishmen who became notorious for this in early nineteenth-century Edinburgh. The verb 'to Burke' a person meant to dig them up after burial. This had to be done within a short time or the body, especially the internal organs, would have decayed too much to be of use to practising surgeons. In this era one poor unfortunate in Dublin died and was buried. Then he was dug up by the Sack 'em Ups who threw him into the Liffey when pursued by the police, from where he was rescued and buried again. So he was buried twice and, in a manner of speaking, drowned, before he got to settle down to his, well earned, eternal rest.

Saints, whether Irish or otherwise, often also went through a period of multiple relocation. There are hundreds of early Irish saints - described as 'saints by acclamation' - acclaimed on account of miracles they performed and the holiness of their lives. Formal Vatican procedures for canonisation were only established in the twelfth century and the first of the very few Irish people to be declared a saint in this way was Laurence O'Toole, Archbishop of Dublin in the twelfth century.

Saints were a source of money for a church or monastery. People would pay a lot to be buried near him or her and this is an additional locational graveyard fact. To this day some people still take a little clay from the reputed grave of a saint for its healing properties. Some major monasteries had thousands of relics. The saint's bones might be dug up and divided among daughter monastic foundations, or the saint's body be boiled up soon after death and the bones separated. It was a major money making enterprise and one of the sources of monastic wealth which attracted the envy of marauding Irish clans, raiding Vikings, and eventually Henry VIII who dissolved almost all English and Irish monasteries in 1538 to 1540.

Often grave gifts were buried with the deceased. The winding sheets of Egyptian mummies have numerous little objects included in them. Sometimes a coin was placed in the hand of the deceased, or under the tongue or on the eyes, as 'admission' money, or a token for Charon to carry them across the River Acheron into the underworld. Even today in Ireland favoured objects are buried with their owners. Not long ago a fishing rod was buried with its owner in Ballyshannon. My friend Margaret McGinley, mother of Sean the actor – in films such as *Braveheart* and *The Field* - placed an obligation or *geis* on me to place a full bottle of whiskey in her coffin or grave, which I did when she was buried on 8 November 1998.

So if, before I started, you thought that after death there was only one great divide – between those who went up and those who went down – I hope I have shown that there might be more locations than you thought!

Notes and references

1 Brian S Turner, 'An observation on settler names in Fermanagh' in *Clogher Record*, vol. viii, no. 3, (1974), pp285-289.

2 Newspaper report, *Impartial Reporter*, Enniskillen, 10 Jan 1867, re enclosure of Killesher and Rossory graveyards.

3 J I D Johnston, *Clogher Cathedral Graveyard* (Clogher 1972).

4 Minutes of the Select Vestry.

Labouring towards the space to belong: identity, locality and the townland in Northern Ireland

Bryonie Reid

The concept of belonging in place acquires particular intricacy in the context of Northern Ireland, where strong territorial imperatives come into intimate conflict. This paper focuses on the locality in Northern Ireland in narratives of place and belonging, arguing that despite its politicisation, it entails at least the possibility of shared and diverse senses of identity. The Townlands Campaign in Northern Ireland provides a case study. The townland's central position in Northern Ireland's rural addresses was largely displaced by road names, house numbers, and postcodes during the 1970s. Community protest emerged and was coordinated into a campaign by members of the Federation for Ulster Local Studies, who continue to address this disruption of place-identity. The campaign is important for its seeming ability to muster support across all elements of Northern Irish society. It provides the basis of a query into whether our senses of localised place may undercut territorial contention at the level of the nation.

'To walk is to lack a place. It is the indefinite process of being absent and in search of a proper . . .': Introduction

(Michel de Certeau, in Sharkey, undated: 29)

It is clear that remembered and current geographical insecurities play a significant part in the Northern Irish conflict. There are severe problems in imagining the six counties as a coherent place; it fits neatly neither into the dominant visions of Ireland as a whole, nor those of Britain, and each of these larger entities is itself increasingly fragmented. The ways in which both unionism and nationalism traditionally construct their claims to the territory of Northern Ireland are centred on absolute ownership and mutual exclusion. Unionist and Protestant narratives of belonging on the land have been couched in terms of suffering and hard work, while nationalist and Catholic narratives have focused on prior settlement and use. This paper aims to uncover alternative means of establishing belonging in place in Northern Ireland. Nuances exist, suspended between and around the simplified narratives; taking into account the ongoing failure of the concept of 'nation' to provide an inclusive or complex ground for belonging in Northern Ireland, the paper focuses on the potential of the locality to do so. Rather than arguing for localities as inherently inclusive of cultural, political and religious diversity in themselves, the concern is with inclusive *uses* and *understandings* of localised space. Unfortunately, many in Northern Ireland place no positive value on inclusion; although these uses of locality could be defined as progressive, that view is not universally shared among unionists and nationalists in the North. However, it seems obvious that some kind of shared belonging needs to be negotiated between the two communities laying claim to the six counties, despite their evident reluctance to do so.

The paper begins by indicating schemes for a Northern Ireland which would be able to transcend national struggles, by being imagined as less than, and more than, a nation. This includes thinking on Northern Ireland as one region of Europe, detached from its national loyalties; as common ground for both nationalist and unionist, different from Britain and Ireland and thus providing shared as well as contested space; and as a 'cultural corridor' between Britain and Ireland (Longley, 1991: 144). A review of the intensely localised nature of 'the Troubles' in Northern Ireland follows, as a challenge to any easy theorising of the local as a solution to the province's opposing belongings.

The argument develops with reference to the case study, the more positive example of the recent use of townlands. Historically, the townland has been a fundamental element of understanding rural and urban space in Ireland, although its place in the address system remained essential only in rural areas. In 1972 the Post Office decided that the townland element of the address was obsolete in Northern Ireland, and would be replaced by house numbers, road names and postcodes. In response, the Townlands Campaign evolved, protesting about this disruption of centuries of identity and belonging in place. The campaign, a ground-level community effort, apparently bypassed the usual frictions and clashes of such issues in Northern Ireland. This is a rare and encouraging example of unity, and of a focus on place and belonging that moves beyond traditional nationalist or unionist concerns. It leads to the contention that uses of Northern Irish localities need not necessarily demonstrate narrow and exclusive definitions of place, belonging and identity, and in fact may provide a significant counterpoint to the rigid and contradictory manifestations of those concepts at the national level. The issue of the eradication of townlands, and the resulting widespread protest, exists in a detailed and ecumenical pattern of belonging woven from diverse localised threads.

The parish and the cosmos: finding local belonging in Northern Ireland

A common analysis of the current global situation, if any analysis pretends to such a broad remit, is that while on the one hand, the world is becoming homogenised and ever more accessible to certain groups, on the other, there is a growing concern with the local, the familiar and the distinctive. It is possible to read this latter phenomenon as a response to the former. Increased mobility (forced or voluntary), competition between various cultures, and the standardising impulse of global capitalism, may all combine to create a sense of dislocation, loss and anxiety, rather than of freedom, progress and choice. Hence the need to preserve difference, and to establish distinctive belonging in community and place at a local level.

Addressing the dichotomy and necessary dialogue between the global and the local in Ireland, Richard Kearney muses on the possibility of a 'fifth province', envisaged as supplement and other to Ireland's existing four, and located at 'the swinging door which connects the "parish" . . . with the "cosmos"' (Kearney, 1997: 100). This concern with opening out attachment to place takes into account the apparent need to be rooted somewhere, but warns against what Neal Ascherson terms a 'black, locked up, excluding sort of provincialism' (Ascherson, 1990: 16). Kearney's notion of the fifth province evolves specifically within the framework of a partitioned Ireland torn by battles to control and define nationhood. Europe, with its long history of racial violence, and its more recent attempts at integration, at some levels is spoken of increasingly in terms of regions rather than of nations, in order to soften the rigidity of borders, and the associated conflicts, across the continent. A regionalised Europe has been welcomed by Kearney as an opportunity to dissipate the Northern Irish conflict by decentralising Britain and Ireland in a way through which Northern Ireland would become one of a 'quasi-autonomous, albeit interconnected' group of regions in the Western European archipelago (Kearney, 1997: 93).

Northern Irish nationalist politician John Hume has interpreted the drive for European unity as suiting both nationalist and unionist aspirations for the province; nationalists may 'take comfort from the fact that an ever closer union applies to both parts of Ireland within Europe', while unionists may focus on 'an ever closer union . . . between Britain and Ireland' in the same framework (Hume, 1996: 126). Pointing out that, in his opinion, in this new Europe of 'multiple' peripheries, and 'diverse' centres, nationalism and unionism may be somewhat anachronistic, he hopes that emphasis on Northern Ireland's wider connections will dissipate its parochial conflict. These theories found an earlier advocate in Ulster poet John Hewitt, the descendant of English Protestant planters. He attempted to respond to the evident need for discourses of belonging in Northern Ireland that would avoid 'a political mystique of Irishness' (Longley, 1992: 19), and provide more cultural depth and authenticity than the traditional British connection. Proposing that Catholic and Protestant could at least consider Northern Ireland shared ground, and base a sense of belonging on their common geographical heritage, Hewitt contextualised that attachment within a wider network of belonging on the island of Ireland, in Britain and in Europe. His democratic vision of belonging was founded on time spent in place and the accumulation of place-based memory, rather than race or religion:

> for we have rights drawn from the soil and sky;
> the use, the pace, the patient years of labour,
> the rain against the lips, the changing light,
> the heavy clay-sucked stride, have altered us;
> we would be strangers in the Capitol;
> this is our country also, nowhere else;
> and we shall not be outcast upon the world.

> (Hewitt, 1991: 79)

A further attempt to envisage Northern Ireland as a shared and distinctive space occurs in Edna Longley's well-known evocation of the province as a 'cultural corridor' (Longley, 1991: 144), in which 'Irishness' and 'Britishness' permeate and alter one another. She pins hope on a culturally hybrid regionalism in literature and other cultural expression, situated within at least two broader contexts (Britain and Ireland); there are echoes here of postcolonial theorist Homi Bhabha's work on the subversive potential of the hybrid, in terms of both space and person (*The Location of Culture*, 1994). He considers that borderline situations and permeable, mongrel identifications implicitly critique the purifying drive of nationalisms and the homogenising drive of global capitalism. However, as Longley acknowledges, unionism and nationalism tend to 'block the corridor at one end . . . [or] the other' (Longley, 1991: 144). Similarly, Hewitt later declared his notion of the distinct and shared space of Northern Ireland a failure, conceding: 'Ulster is not one region, it's several regions . . . My concept of regionalism was trying to bring together incompatible pieces' (in McDonald, 1995: 45). Hewitt's theories stumbled over Northern Ireland's real and minutely scaled geographical differentiation, and likewise, Bhabha's theories present certain problems when contextualised in actuality. Katharyne Mitchell believes that Bhabha's premise almost re-essentialises liminal spaces and characters, in that he supposes them *inevitably* to enshrine resistance (Mitchell, 1997). Those criticisms may be applied to any suggestion that localities are subversive in themselves rather than in their uses. Mitchell argues that borderline spaces, given their existence in 'real' geography and history, could as easily become spaces of 'closure and cultural homogenization', as has clearly occurred in Northern Ireland.

'That determined place': the challenge of sectarian geography

(W. R. Rodgers, in McDonald, 1995: 58)

The presentation of the local as an alternative to national allegiances (and hence conflicts) in Northern Ireland is seductive. However, the elevation of the local as a space that transcends constitutional questions and essentialisms faces a glaring difficulty, which is that, all too often, it does nothing of the kind. Northern Ireland may be described as an intermingled, borderland area, but this context has resulted more often in fossilisation of identity and difference than any kind of acceptance, let alone celebration of, ambiguity. The province's sectarian politics historically extend to geography, and the last thirty years in particular have been characterised by further polarisation of settlement. Areas that may at first glance seem to be mixed often simply break down into more and more intricate segregation, which is reinforced time and again in response to violence. A. T. Q. Stewart sums up the problem as follows:

> the two communities are not intermingled . . . but they are interlocked . . . This gives rise to a situation in which the 'territorial imperative' is extremely insistent . . . the war in Ulster is being fought out on a narrower ground than even the most impatient observer might imagine, a ground every inch of which has its own associations and special meaning . . . locality and history are welded together.

(Stewart, 1977: 181-182).

Communities have painfully learned the risks of living alongside the 'other'; Susan McKay cites several cases of sectarian murder involving Catholics and Protestants from the same locality, using this situation to question unreflective tendencies to value localised integration (McKay, 2000). Territorial localisation in Belfast is now such that distrust between neighbouring Protestant communities matches that between adjoining Protestant and Catholic areas. David Holloway indicates in an essay on the Protestant Donegall Pass in Belfast that the boundaries are now being drawn at a smaller scale than ever:

> I was confronted with a community that had a clear sense of geographical separation and a strong identity [sic] from all the surrounding communities, in terms of rivalry, antagonism and mistrust, regardless of religion. For the people of the Donegall Pass, there was no blurring of the boundaries.

(Holloway, 1994: 9).

Belonging within national discourses is fraught with contradiction and characterised by simplification and selective amnesia. Belonging within local discourses can be equally oppositional, fragmented, and traumatic, yet it contains the potential to complicate sectarian models. An unassuming example of this potential occurs in the Townlands Campaign, providing a surprising counterpoint to the usual political acrimony. Faced with the threat of townland names and boundaries disappearing from use and memory in Northern Ireland, Protestants and Catholics have marshalled consistent and voluble protest, both separately and together. The spaces and their names, abundant in their associations with local identity and belonging, seem to be largely considered as a shared resource and heritage. In its working from the ground up, so to speak, the campaign provides a litmus test for theories of local inclusion, a prism which acts to reflect and deconstruct abstract conjecture.

'The child's open-eyed attention to the small and the familiar': the Townlands Campaign

(Heaney, 1980: 142)

A history of the Townlands Campaign

The townland is one of the most basic units of land division in Ireland, 'the most intimate and enduring' (Ó Dalaigh et al, 1998: 9). The first official evidence of their existence occurs in church records from before the twelfth century (Muhr, 1999: 5), and thereafter they appear in all legal documents pertaining to land usage and ownership. As a sanctioned form of understanding Irish land division and naming, most of these spaces and names were preserved practically untouched throughout the vagaries of the Plantation years. Across Ireland the townland retained its historical function in administrative and legal circles, its position confirmed as the principal element of rural addresses. However, in Northern Ireland in 1972 the Post Office initiated the now current system of using road names, numbers, and postcodes, citing increased efficiency and speed of delivery to rural addresses. Nonetheless, most communities deemed road names and numbers and postcodes unacceptable.

One road with one name may cut through several townlands, and road names could be assigned with no reference to local names and in ignorance of local opinions and knowledge. Townland names weren't banned, but were considered 'superfluous information' (Kirk-Smith, 1993: 46), and people were requested not to include them on addresses.

Objections were voiced almost unanimously across the province. However, local authorities were the government bodies responsible for validating such a change, and as the structures of local government were undergoing alterations at this time, in the confusion the Post Office's directive was 'allowed . . . to become law, almost by default' (McCool, 1993). To date Fermanagh is the only county which managed to resist the scheme completely, although coming under great pressure to conform.

Towards the mid-1970s, a campaign to rescind the Post Office's guidelines was launched through the Federation for Ulster Local Studies, an umbrella organisation for the province's local historical societies. The Federation perceived a need to coordinate a response and reassure people of their townland's validity. If the names fell into disuse, they and the exact spaces to which they referred would certainly be forgotten. The initial reaction was one of outrage that a structure of names and spaces that had such a lengthy history in the community was to be discarded for the Post Office's convenience. As Kay Muhr points out, 'the townland was for centuries the building block of local society' (Muhr, 1999: 3), and it came as a shock to have those building blocks of identity and belonging summarily tumbled down. Although the Post Office lacked the power to make the townland names illegal, its discouragement of their use gave some rural dwellers that impression; anxious that cheques and other official post should be able to reach them, the Post Office's directive was often followed despite protest. The Federation's first statement on the matter, published in its journal in 1976, warned that:

> the Post Office system, where implemented, is leading to the disuse of the townland name, firstly by official bodies, and then by members of the public who are made to feel that there is something improper or unreliable about its use.

(Federation for Ulster Local Studies, 1976: 21)

The meaning of the Townlands Campaign

The evidently strong desire among communities in Northern Ireland to protect local distinctiveness from the globalising imperative is important. Townlands, while not exceptional in the sense that similar small land divisions would have been known elsewhere in Europe, are uniquely long-lived. This framework, an integral part of spatialised identity in Ireland for almost a millenium, is a prime example of the geographical scale in which E. Estyn Evans considers 'the most genuine bonds' to form between person and place (Evans, 1967: 8). These small, 'pragmatic' units (Ó Dalaigh et al, 1998: 10), are redolent of an attachment to place which is both crumbling and petrifying in the wake of increasing homogenisation. Nonetheless, the understanding of identity and belonging that emanates from townland-measured orientation in place can be both modest and far-reaching. The attack on this form of local grounding elicits frequent expressions of distress in the available literature, one example being Joe McCool's belief that:

> the townland is at the heart of rural thought . . . the loss will be not only of a sonorous beauty and historical sense but also a corruption of the intimate relationship between rural people and the land that surrounds them.

(McCool, 1993)

Ian Kirk-Smith ascribes 'psychological and moral' meanings to the townland in this context. Rather than providing the impulse for a merely narrow and nostalgic celebration of the local, 'while a tidal wave of international culture sweeps inexorably across the land, conquering and absorbing the local, the townland has been at the centre of a campaign of resistance' (Kirk-Smith, 1993: 46). The simple act of paying attention to 'the eclectic and the ordinary ... [to] local particularity in a context of universal process', a quality of Evans' work in which Brian Graham finds contemporary resonance (Graham, 1994: 198), can perhaps act in itself as an antidote both to the destruction and the exploitation of a sense of belonging in place. Seamus Heaney too has lauded the power of the local:

> empowered within its own horizon, it looks out but does not necessarily look up to the metropolitan centres . . . it is self-sufficient but not self-absorbed, capable of thought: undaunted, pristine, spontaneous: a corrective to the inflations of nationalism and the cringe of provincialism.

(in Canavan, 1991: xi)

Indeed, it may form the foundation of a more gentle, careful, and free-ranging thinking than does a rootless universal perspective. Catherine Nash recognises and questions the 'tendency to celebrate hybridity over authenticity, dislocation over location, mobility over rootedness' (Nash, 1999, 471); rather, the importance of both depends on their dialogue.

The potential of townlands to resist homogenising bureaucracy extends further. A fundamental objection to road names and numbers that involved the disruption of an ancient understanding of place in Ireland was put succinctly by Joe McCool; 'a townland is an area, it is not a long thin thing called a road' (in McGurk, 1993). In 1977 Brian Turner had stated: 'we feel [the Post Office scheme] is destroying the pattern of knowledge associated with the townland system' (Turner, 1977b: 24). This pattern of knowledge and memory is spatially oriented, rather than linear. In reference to Northern Irish space, the replacement of the townland system with the road system echoes early Elizabethan administrative strategies in Ireland. Andrew Hadfield and Willy Maley describe early modern Ireland as 'both a mirror and hammer' (Bradshaw et al, 1993: 15) in relation to English identity; while its colonisers and governors attempted to define themselves by moulding Ireland into their Other, its 'complex, differentiated, heterogeneous and variegated' nature repeatedly shattered that image. Hence the persistent attempts at control through mapping, where land and inhabitants could be textually ordered and categorised, and brought under the power of the gaze. However, David Baker points out that as the Irish often only recognised English borders in order to weight their incursion with meaning, 'colonial "plotting" embodies just as much the disturbance of its own categories as their establishment . . . it declares itself a ceaselessly violated invention' (Baker, 1993: 88).

It could be argued that a similar process is occurring in the imposition of linear geography over an already existing spatial mode of orientation. This 'thick' space (see Herr, 1996) entails the possibility of resistance to reorganisation from above, as thoroughly enmeshed as it has been with human life and death. In the context of the limited and inflexible definitions of belonging in place and community in Northern Ireland, townlands and their names represent the possibility that the locality involves multifaceted and dishevelled stories of identity and belonging, although these may not necessarily be recovered; they also bear the distinction of lengthy use and association. Road names have proved ultimately unsatisfactory not least because they have not 'evolve[d] naturally from within the community' (Turner, 1977a: 26), and inadequately represent local identity and belonging.

Central to the Townlands Campaign's importance in this context is its apparent ability to garner support across communities. The literature makes frequent reference to this characteristic, often mentioned almost as an aside rather than as the campaign's main ethos. Hence there are comments such as 'support for our position has been virtually unanimous and has come from many different kinds of people' (Turner, 1977a: 26), and 'townlands belong to us all . . . they are part of our shared heritage' (Federation for Ulster Local Studies, undated). In several places it is mentioned that the issue of preserving the townland system proved to be a uniting force for Fermanagh District Council, unusually enough in its history, and elsewhere it is noted that the idea to include townland names on road signs apparently originated with an Orangeman (see Carroll, 1996; Kirk-Smith, 1993; Muhr, 2002). It seems that the origins of townlands and their names may not be a matter of contention or even importance to many of the campaigners; for them the spaces' value lies in their protracted use and human associations, in their links with the past and their stories about landscape and settlers. Of course, townlands are as vulnerable to assimilation into conventional religio-political geographies as any other space, and can be subject to the same levels of prejudiced perception, justified and unjustified, particularly when it comes promoting their linguistic significance. On the other hand, explored without political nuances, the literal meaning of townland names can provide not only factual information but cultural illumination and linkages to a wide audience.

Catherine Nash writes of the Townlands Campaign as a refreshing rethinking of attachment to place in the Northern Irish context, as people unite against the 'common threat' (Nash, 1999: 469) of bureaucratised nomenclature and construction of place. If local knowledges can supplant the discourses of nationality and religion when speaking of belonging in place, the notion could be opened out, a step which the Townlands Campaign seems to be making at times, whether consciously or not. This process is resonant of Hewitt's understanding of belonging, in which time creates attachment to place and allows roots to be put down, eventually making no distinction between planter and native. As Seamus Heaney writes in his introduction to *Every Stoney Acre has a Name*:

> the associations of the word [townland] are rural, of course, but I suspect that its talismanic power is felt by city people also . . . it connotes a totally uninsistent sense of difference, a freely espoused relation to an idiom and an identity that are regional, authentic, uncoerced and acknowledged. It is a minimal but reliable shared possession, the kind of word that could provide the right verbal foundation for talks about talks.

(in Canavan, 1991: xi)

Despite the largely shared interest in townlands in rural areas, and although Heaney reminds us that townlands as spatial divisions exist in cities also, the localised territorial patterns of urban conflict warn against placing too much hope in the reconciliatory potential of local attachment. Belfast's streets and townlands continue to be violently and rigorously segregated, clearly evident in the fierce conflict in 2001 between the neighbouring areas of the Short Strand and the Lower Newtownards Road. Perhaps the most to be said for the use of townlands in this context is that they are at least a common way of understanding Belfast's divided geography.

However, the overwhelming tenor of the interest in townlands has been inclusive and preservative in nature, the emphasis being on an existing mongrel heritage rather than the creation or recovery of a pure one. There is also no constitutional question in the balance, whatever the outcome of the campaign. It seems to have survived largely unco-opted by unionism or nationalism, working beneath and beyond their more elevated and more limited concerns. The failure of the local to open out in urban areas is a serious drawback to generalised theory on its progressive possibilities. Its power, where it exists in positive form, is something indefinable, ordinary, unassuming and easily missed, something sufficiently fragile that, if made to bear the burdens of Peace or Identity, may crumble. A grand solution to the geographical attritions of Northern Ireland seems unlikely, but a beginning may be made through the use of townlands in observing, drawing attention to, and participating in the rich web of names and spaces we inherit from the various past.

'The anthology of memories of the other is a book I hadn't reckoned on . . .': Conclusion

(Ian Crichton Smith, in Falconer, 1998: 13)

This web of spaces spatially and imaginatively divides Northern Ireland into individual localities, at various scales. At some level, many have a stated political, cultural or religious identity, no matter their actual or historical diversity. This situation emanates from the lack of an overarching, embracing narrative of place to which all inhabitants of Northern Ireland may subscribe, and in part explains how it has failed conceptually as a geographical entity in its own right. Seamus Heaney highlights the difficulties of such competing constructions of place-identity as do exist:

> the fountainhead of the Unionist's myth springs in the Crown of England but he has to hold his own on the island of Ireland. The fountainhead of the Nationalist's myth lies in the idea of an integral Ireland, but he too lives in exile from his ideal place.
>
> (Heaney, 1984: 5)

This dual geographic understanding of Northern Ireland has been an integral part of its conflict, creating 'the strain of being in two places at once' (Heaney, 1984: 5). There have been various attempts to resolve or to dissolve the problem. Resolutions have often been couched in terms of being able to prove prior possession and hence authenticity; the nationalist and republican movements have until recently gone unchallenged in their use of the Irish-Ireland myths. Now some unionists and loyalists are beginning to reciprocate, creating Ulster Scots myths to vindicate their presence in Northern Ireland through prehistory, language and naming place; this constitutes an attempt to fix Protestant belonging in the north of Ireland as 'immemorial and uncontrollable' (Foster, 1988: 78).

That there are deep problems of belonging in place and remembering in Northern Ireland cannot and should not be denied. There are, however, different stories that emerge quietly beneath the close look, which enable, with effort, a kind of remembering which questions established boundaries and oppositions. Localities investigated on an intimate scale will reveal selective and sectarian modes of remembering, belonging, and identifying, but there will also exist counter-memories, belongings, and identities. Beneath the coarse political certainties lies a finer, more variegated pattern, which encompasses the larger structure, but is not defined by it. Rather than the 'abstractly conceived whole, the cosmos . . . the rationalistic preoccupation with the universal' (Val Plumwood, in Davion, 1994: 15), the particular should be attended to, provided the attention accepts disharmony and fallibility at that level as at all others. Its advantage lies in its scope to record more detailed, and usually more complex experiences. Pat Loughrey imagines townland names as 'the index-cards upon which memories were stored' (Loughrey, 1986: 211), and these small index-cards may be a way of remembering more hopefully in Northern Ireland, moving from what Edna Longley calls 'cynical, selective forgetting', to 'responsible, alarming memory' (Longley, 2001: 253).

Belonging in its geographical manifestation is an integral part of Northern Ireland's flimsily constructed polarisations, but one that could contain a latent possibility of dismantling these polarisations. The townland in itself has no inherently inclusive qualities; in fact, it could be argued that localities are inherently *ex*clusive, through the very act of defining them as one place and not another. However, the interpretations to which townlands have been subjected through the Townlands Campaign demonstrate an awareness of the complex texture of local spaces, a texture that can make partisan simplification difficult. This is not to claim that the Townlands Campaign is the key to achieving peace; its importance here resides in its sidestepping of such universals.

Tom Clyde compares John Hewitt's work on Ulster's forgotten histories to that of a farmer on an overgrown field, 'clearing away the undergrowth of lies and amnesia. . . as groundwork for the future, a way of clearing weeds and encouraging healthy growth' (Clyde, 1987: viii). The analogy ascribes value to the patient and persistent exposure of Northern Ireland's real historical multiplicity. This may be done effectively at the level of the local, although local studies do not inevitably entail such disruption of the dominant religious, ethnic, and political narratives. For this reason the local should not be theorised as a solution to Northern Ireland's sectarian conflict. Its uses, as evidenced by the Townlands Campaign, may possibly form, rather, a clearing, a reversed palimpsest, a 'thick' space in which certainties are complicated, and things forgotten aired. This paper argues that to root historical variety in geographical locality provides the common environment that permits dialogue between forms of belonging. Rooted and tangled memories linger in local places, shaping identity and belonging; perhaps obscured, tarnished through disuse or grief, but awaiting careful excavation, examination and reinstatement in the record of what has gone before; if not a panacea, at least a facet of a challenge to today's sectarian simplicities.

References

Ascherson, Neil (June 1990), 'The Four Motors are Driving Off', *Fortnight*, 296, 16-19.
Baker, David (1993), 'Off the Map: Charting Uncertainty in Renaissance Ireland', in Bradshaw, B., Hadfield, A. and Maley, W. (eds.) *Representing Ireland: Literature and the Origins of Conflict, 1534-1660* (Cambridge), pp76-92.
Bhabha, Homi (1994), *The Location of Culture* (London and New York).
Bradshaw, B, Hadfield, A, Maley, W (eds.) (1993), *Representing Ireland: Literature and the Origins of Conflict, 1534-1660* (Cambridge).
Canavan, Tony (ed.) (1991), *Every Stoney Acre has a Name: a Celebration of the Townland in Ulster* (Belfast).
Carroll, R (1996), 'Townlands they Love so Well', *Irish News*, 8th April.
Clyde, Tom (ed.) (1987) *Ancestral Voices: the Selected Prose of John Hewitt* (Belfast and Wolfeboro,New Hampshire).
Davion, V (1994), 'Is Ecofeminism Feminist?', in Warren, K. (ed.) *Ecological Feminism* (London and New York), pp8-28.
Evans, E Estyn (1967), *The Irishness of the Irish*, paper given at the Annual Gathering of the Irish Association, Armagh, 22nd September.
Falconer, Alan (1998), 'Remembering', in Falconer, A. and Liechty, J. (eds.) *Reconciling Memories* (Dublin), 11-19.
Federation for Ulster Local Studies (1976), 'The Post Office and Rural Addresses in Northern Ireland – a Federation Statement', Ulster Local Studies, 2(1), November, 21-23.
Federation for *Ulster Local Studies* (undated), 'Townlands: a User's Guide', informal publicity material.

Foster, Roy (1988), *Modern Ireland*: 1600-1972 (London).

Graham, Brian (1994), 'No Place of the Mind: Contested Protestant Representations of Ulster' in *Ecumene*, 1(3), 257-281.

Heaney, Seamus (1980), *Preoccupations: Selected Prose 1968-1978* (London and Boston).

Heaney, Seamus (1984), *Place and Displacement: Recent Poetry of Northern Ireland* (Grasmere).

Herr, Cheryl (1996), *Critical Regionalism and Cultural Studies: from Ireland to the American Mid-West* (Gaineville,Florida).

Hewitt, John (1991), *The Collected Poems of John Hewitt* (Belfast).

Holloway, David (1994), 'Territorial Aspects, Cultural Identity: the Protestant Community of Donegall Pass, Belfast', *Causeway*, Winter, 9-12.

Hume, John (1996), *Personal Views: Politics, Peace and Reconciliation in Ireland* (Dublin).

Kearney, Richard (1997) *Postnationalist Ireland: Politics, Culture, Philosophy* (London and New York).

Kirk-Smith, Ian (1993), 'Going Local', *Fortnight*, 315, March, 46.

Longley, Edna (1991), 'Opening Up: a New Pluralism', in Johnstone, R. and Wilson, R. (eds.) *Troubled Times: Fortnight Magazine and the Troubles in Northern Ireland 1970-1991* (Belfast), pp141-144.

Longley, Edna (1992), 'Writing, Revisionism and Grass-Seed: Literary Mythologies in Ireland', in Lundy, J. and Mac Póilin, A. (eds.) *Styles of Belonging: the Cultural Identities of Ulster* (Belfast), pp11-21.

Longley, Edna (2001), 'Northern Ireland: Commemoration, Elegy, Forgetting', in McBride, I. (ed.) *History and Memory in Modern Ireland* (Cambridge).

Loughrey, Patrick (1986), 'Communal Identity in Rural Northern Ireland', in *Ulster Local Studies*, Autumn, 205-211.

McCool, Joe (1993), 'Last Chance to Save Townland', *Belfast Newsletter*, 9th February.

McDonald, Peter (1995) 'The Fate of 'Identity': John Hewitt, W. R. Rodgers, and Louis MacNeice', in Patten, E. (ed.), *Returning to Ourselves: the Second Volume of Papers from the John Hewitt International Summer School* (Belfast), pp41-60.

McGurk, J (1993), 'Crusade to Save Ancient Names of Townlands Gathers Strength', *Irish News*, 4th March.

McKay, Susan (2000), *Northern Protestants: an Unsettled People* (Belfast).

Mitchell, Katharyne (1997) 'Different Diasporas and the Hype of Hybridity', *Environment and Planning D: Society and Space*, 15(3), 533-553.

Muhr, Kay (1999), *Celebrating Ulster's Townlands: a Place-Name Exhibition for the Millennium* (Belfast).

Muhr, Kay (2002), 'Townland News: a Report on the Work of the Ulster Place Name Society', *Due North*, 1(5), Spring/Summer, 16-18.

Nash, Catherine (1999), 'Irish Place Names: Postcolonial Locations', in *Transactions (Institute of British Geographers)*, 24(4), 457-481.

Ó Dálaigh, Brian, Cronin, Denis, and Connell, Paul (eds.) (1998) *Irish Townlands: Essays in Local History* (Dublin).

Sharkey, Sabina (undated), 'Of Salt, Song, Stone and Marrow-bone: the Work of Anne Tallentire', in Connor, V. (ed.) *Anne Tallentire* (exhibition catalogue), (Dublin), pp25-40.

Stewart, A T Q (1977), *The Narrow Ground: Aspects of Ulster 1609-1969* (London).

Turner, Brian S (1977a), 'The Post Office and Rural Addresses', in *Ulster Local Studies*, 2(2), May, 26-27.

Turner, Brian S (1977b), 'Federation News: Secretary's Report 1976-1977', in *Ulster Local Studies*, 3(1), November, 23-26.

Notes on Contributors

Stan Brown of Carnreagh, Hillsborough, County Down, is Business Development Director for the Ordnance Survey of Northern Ireland.

John Cunningham of The Commons, Belleek, County Fermanagh, is a retired schoolteacher, a local historian and professional tour guide, and trustee of the Ulster Local History Trust.

Cahal Dallat of Ballycastle, County Antrim, is a retired school principal, a local historian, President of the John Hewitt International Summer School, and past chairman of the Ulster Local History Trust.

Patrick Duffy, from Cremartin, Castleblayney, County Monaghan, is Professor of Geography at Maynooth College, National University of Ireland.

Patrick Fitzgerald of Letfern, Seskinore, County Tyrone, is an historian, lecturer and development officer at the Centre for Migration Studies at the Ulster-American Folk Park, Castletown, Omagh, County Tyrone.

Bryan Gallagher of Drumclay, Enniskillen, County Fermanagh, is a retired school principal and an author and broadcaster.

Myrtle Hill of Ballyhenry, Newtownabbey, County Antrim, is an historian, head of the Centre for Women's Studies at Queen's University, Belfast, and chairman of the Ulster Local History Trust.

Jack Johnston from Ratory, Clogher, County Tyrone, is a farmer and historian, and past chairman of the Ulster Local History Trust.

Brian Lambkin of Ballynafeigh, Belfast, is Director of the Centre for Migration Studies at the Ulster-American Folk Park, Castletown, Omagh, County Tyrone, and Chairman of the Association of European Migration Institutions.

Patrick Loughrey from Ray, Rathmullan, County Donegal, is Director of Nations and Regions for the British Broadcasting Corporation, and a trustee of the Ulster Local History Trust.

Eugene McCabe of Drumard, Clones, County Monaghan, is a farmer, novelist, short story writer, and playwright for both stage and television.

Patrick McKay from Gortagharn, Randalstown, County Antrim is a research fellow with the Northern Ireland Place-Name Project and secretary of the Ulster Place-Name Society.

Tess Maginess from Annaghbeg, Killyman, County Tyrone, has worked in rural arts and community development, and is a writer, and a tutor and student support officer at the Armagh campus of Queen's University.

Annesley Malley of Drumahoe, County Londonderry, is a retired chartered surveyor and land agent, a local historian, and trustee of the Ulster Local History Trust.

Emer Ní Cheallaigh from Finglas, Dublin, is an archivist and collector in the Department of Irish Folklore, University College, Dublin.

Bryonie Reid from Ballymenagh, Holywood, County Down, is a postgraduate student at the Academy for Irish Cultural Heritages, University of Ulster at Magee.

Wendy Swan from Monery, Crossdoney, County Cavan, is a retired farmer and a volunteer guide at the Church of Ireland Cathedral of St Fethlimidh, Kilmore.

Brian Turner of Lisban, Saul, County Down, is a consultant in museums and historical interpretation, secretary of the Irish National Committee of the International Council of Museums, and a trustee of the Ulster Local History Trust.

Registered conference participants

Allen, Stanley, Newtownards, co. Down
Baird, Albert, Lisdalgan, co. Down
Baird, Mabel, Lisdalgan, co. Down
Black, Lynn, Ballymena, co. Antrim
Brady, Oliver, Cloneary, co. Cavan
Brown, Stan, Carnreagh, co. Down
Brown, June, The Glen, Monaghan
Brown, Maureen, Portadown, co. Armagh
Callaghan, Jimmy, Roslea, co. Fermanagh
Carr, Peter, Belfast
Cassidy, Patrick, Cootehill, co. Cavan
Comey, Michael, Cavan
Connolly, Michael, Stranoodan, co. Monaghan
Corcoran, Doreen, Greenisland, co. Antrim
Cunningham, John B, The Commons, Belleek, co. Fermanagh
Cusack, Catherina M, Killymeehan, co. Cavan
D'Arcy, Patricia, Lisnabrinia, co. Cavan
Dallat, Dr Cahal, Ballycastle, co. Antrim
De Breadun, Una, Rosinver, co. Leitrim
Dolan, Philomena
Dolan, Mary, Drummacoorin, co. Fermanagh
Dolan, Micheal, Drummacoorin, co. Fermanagh
Donoghue, Freda, Virginia, co. Cavan
Doran, John, Corleanamaddy, co. Monaghan
Duffy, Professor Patrick, Maynooth, co. Kildare
Duffy, Malcolm, Aughnacloy, co. Tyrone
Evans, Stephen, Belfast
Fitzgerald, Dr Patrick, Letfern, co. Tyrone
Fitzpatrick, Declan, Derravona, co. Cavan,
Flynn, Betty, Gallonbawn, co. Cavan,
Gallagher, Bryan, Drumclay, co. Fermanagh
Galligan, Doris, Kilnaleck, co. Cavan
Galligan, Sean, Lisnalee, co. Cavan
Gardiner, Ann, Drumnacanvy, co. Armagh
Gibson, Vera E, Cloonaveel, co. Fermanagh
Gordan-McBride, Mary
Hagan, Felix Anthony, Pomeroy, co. Tyrone
Hannon, Joan, Cootehill, co. Cavan
Hammond, David, Belfast

David Hammond singing
Felix Kearney's ballad, The
hills above Drumquin.

Herbert, Vicky, Lisnaskea, co. Fermanagh
Hill, Dr Myrtle, Ballyhenry, co. Antrim
Hillan, Sophia, Belfast
Holland, Pat, Carrickmacross, co. Monaghan
Johnston, Jack, Ratory, co.Tyrone
Kane, Betty, Tullylish, co. Monaghan
Keaney, Maureen, Clooneer, co. Leitrim
Kelly, Eileen, Calry, Sligo
Kennedy, P J, Quivvy, co. Cavan,
Lambkin, Dr Brian, Ballynafeigh, Belfast
Leddy, Anthony, CMRD, Ballyhaise, co. Cavan
Lewis, Margaret, Coolshannagh, Monaghan
Loughrey, Patrick, Kew, Surrey, England
Maginess, Dr Tess, Annaghbeg, co. Tyrone
Maguire, Anne, Derrylea, co. Fermanagh
Maguire, Dermot, Derrylea, co. Fermanagh
Maguire, James, Ederny, co. Fermanagh
Maguire, Dr Marie, Portora, co. Fermanagh
Malley, Annesley, Drumahoe, co. Londonderry
Markey, Eugene, Ballyjamesduff, co. Cavan
Masterson, Una
McAdam, Allen, CMRD, Ballyhaise, co. Cavan
McAdam, Peadar
McCabe, Aidan, Coolshannagh, co. Monaghan
McCabe, Brian, Johnstown, co. Kildare
McCabe, Eugene, Drumard, co. Monaghan
McCabe, John, Drumgoon, co. Cavan
McCaffrey, Oliver, Roslea, co. Fermanagh
McCannon, Jim, Mullinahinch, co. Monaghan
McCaughery, Michael, Monaghan
McCaughey, Josephine, Clogher, co. Tyrone
MacCinna, Nora, Muineachan
McClelland, Ann, Portadown, co. Armagh
McCord, Elizabeth, Killyvilly, co. Fermanagh
McDermott, Larry, Dunogue, co. Monaghan
McGinnity, Annie, Roslea, co. Fermanagh
McGrath, Niamh, CMRD, Ballyhaise, co. Cavan
McKay, Dr. Patrick, Belfast
McKenna, Eileen, Monaghan
McKenna, Maria, Monaghan
McKenna, Patricia, Brackagh, co. Monaghan
McKittrick, Joan, Tandragee, co. Armagh
McMahon, Jim, Leitrim, co. Monaghan

Vicky Herbert at her bookstall.

MacMahon, Theo, Tully, Monaghan
McManus, Sean, co. Down
Meehan, Majella, Monaghan
Moen, Phyllis, Lisglasson, co. Monaghan
Montgomery, Alex, Castleblayney, co. Monaghan
Montgomery, George, Latton, co. Monaghan
Montgomery, Nixon, Latton , co. Monaghan
Morrissey, George, Belturbet, co. Cavan
Mulligan, Ann, Roslea, co. Fermanagh
Mullin, Larry, Ballinode, co. Sligo
Murnane, Peadar, Ballybay, co. Monaghan
Murphy, Kevin, Carricknagavna, co. Armagh
Ní Cheallaigh, Emer, Dublin
Nallan, Maura, Cullies, Cavan
Nicholson, Dorothea, Derryogue, co. Down
Nicholson, Samuel, Derryogue, co. Down
Nulty, Colette, Monaghan
Ó Dincin, Alfai, Muineachan
Ó Dincin, Phil, Muineachan
O'Donnell, Mary, Enniskillen, co. Fermanagh
O'Higgins, Josephine, Aghintamy, co. Monaghan
Ó Luana, Seosamh, Cloghereragh, co. Sligo
O'Reilly, Ciaran, Ballyjamesduff, co. Cavan
O'Reilly, Eileen, Annagh, co. Cavan,
O'Reilly, Rita, Tirkeenan, co. Monaghan,
Ó Riordáin, Séan, Bailieborough, co. Cavan,
Pollock, Vera, Drumlion, co. Cavan,
Reid, Bryonie, Belfast
Reihill, John James, Inniscorkish, co. Fermanagh
Ruth, Bernie, Monaghan
Savage, Jerome, Carrickaderry, co. Monaghan
Scoil Mhuire, Clontibret (Rang a sé)
Sloan, Gary, Open University
Smith, Thomas, Cavan
Smyth, Eileen, Roslea, co. Fermanagh
Smyth Maura, Nolagh, co. Cavan
Steenson, Graham, Monaghan
Steenson, Elizabeth, Monaghan
Stevenson, Valerie E, co. Down
Swan, Wendy, Monery, co. Cavan
Traynor, Peadar, Monaghan
Treanor, Barney, Tongfahan, co. Monaghan
Turner, Dr Brian, Lisban, co. Down
Turner, Helen, Lisban, co. Down
Walsh, Una, Carricknagavna, co. Armagh
Woods, Mary, Aughnameena, Monaghan

*Theo MacMahon
chairing a session.*

The Cavan-Monaghan Rural Development Co-op Society

Cavan-Monaghan Rural Development Co-operative Society empowers individuals and communities to work towards the sustainable economic, social, environmental, cultural and heritage development of their areas.

The Society has been in operation since 1991, promoting and encouraging rural development in the counties of Cavan and Monaghan, a border region which has suffered economically and socially due, among other factors, to political division and conflict. The company is currently delivering the Irish National Rural Development Programme 2002-2006.

Since 1991 CMRD has drawn down or been associated with the investment of millions of euro in the region under the European Union LEADER I and LEADER II programmes and other initiatives that it has undertaken. Under LEADER II alone, the Society has been responsible for the creation of over 200 full-time jobs in the region.

In addition to direct funding of projects, the Society has been responsible for supporting the establishment and development of over 180 local groups. This support has greatly enhanced the ability of local people to become directly involved in problem-solving and development work in their own areas. The assistance provided by LEADER has in turn enabled many of these groups to access funding from other agencies operating in the region. Additionally, under LEADER II training programmes over 2,000 people have been trained in areas such as computers, tourism marketing, facilitation skills, small business development and rural development. The Society has also established sectoral sub-groups in the areas of tourism, heritage, women's development, crafts, agriculture and food.

Contact information:

By post:
Cavan-Monaghan Rural Development Co-op Society
The Agricultural College
Ballyhaise
County Cavan

By electronic mail:
cmrd@iol.ie

Web site:
www.cmrd.ie

The Ulster Local History Trust

The Ulster Local History Trust is dedicated to raising standards and promoting innovation in the voluntary local history movement within the nine counties of Ulster.

Patron: Seamus Heaney

Trustees: Doreen Corcoran, John Cunningham, Cahal Dallat, David Harkness, Myrtle Hill, Jack Johnston, Patrick Loughrey, Malachy McGrady, Theo McMahon, Annesley Malley, Lord O'Neill, Brian Turner.

The Trust is an independent voluntary and charitable body established by the Federation for Ulster Local Studies to help raise the standard of local historical work, particularly among voluntary groups, and to assert its relevance in our society. In the last decade it has supported over 100 local history projects.

The trust has the nine counties of Ulster as its area of primary concern and this deliberate policy is intended to emphasise both inclusiveness and a willingness to recognise that difference can be respected and welcomed rather than feared. The trustees believe that the study of our history on a human scale carries not only personal interest for the individual, but can get to the heart of many of the questions which challenge our sense of identity and cultural confidence in the modern world.

Contact information:

By post:
Ulster Local History Trust
PO Box 900
Downpatrick
County Down BT30 6EF

By electronic mail:
ulht@ulht.org

Web site:
www.ulht.org